100 PAINTINGS

RENARD PRESS – PLAYSCRIPT IV

100 PAINTINGS: ORIGINAL PERFORMANCE AT BREAD AND ROSES THEATRE IN 2021, WITH THE ARTIST PLAYED BY CONRAD WILLIAMSON, THE MOTHER PLAYED BY CATHERINE MCDONOUGH, BEATRIZ PLAYED BY JANE CHRISTIE AND EVA PLAYED BY JILL PENFOLD, DIRECTED BY ZACHARY HART, PRODUCED BY MIHNEA SAVUICA.

ORIGINAL PRODUCTION AT THE HOPE THEATRE IN 2022, DIRECTED BY ZACHARY HART, PRODUCED BY MIHNEA SAVUICA, DESIGNED BY ZSOFIA SAROSI. THE ARTIST PLAYED BY CONRAD WILLIAMSON, THE MOTHER PLAYED BY DENISE STEPHENSON, BEATRIZ PLAYED BY JANE CHRISTIE AND EVA PLAYED BY JULIET GARRICKS.

SPECIAL THANKS TO LEONORA NICHOLSON, JACK WHITNEY, PHIL BARTLETT, LIZ BACON, ELLIE WALKER-SMITH, LITTLE WINDMILL PRODUCTIONS LTD AND JASMINE WILLIAMS.

100 PAINTINGS

JACK MICHAEL STACEY

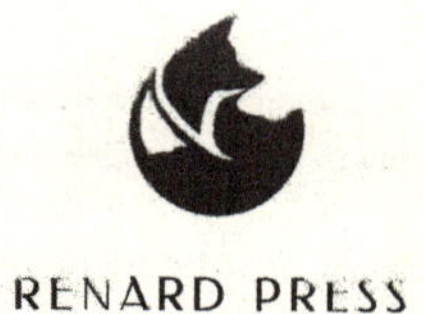

RENARD PRESS

RENARD PRESS LTD

Kemp House
152–160 City Road
London EC1V 2NX
United Kingdom
info@renardpress.com
020 8050 2928

www.renardpress.com

100 Paintings first published by Renard Press Ltd in 2022

Printed in the United Kingdom by Severn

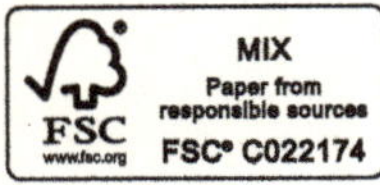

ISBN: 978-1-80447-012-1

9 8 7 6 5 4 3 2 1

CONTENTS

100 PAINTINGS

FOR MUM AND DAD,
WHO HAVE ALWAYS SUPPORTED MY
POOR CAREER CHOICES.

'There is no final one; revolutions are infinite.'
YEVGENY ZAMYATIN, We

CHARACTERS

THE ARTIST

THE MOTHER, *a proud woman with a presence that could never go unnoticed*

BEATRIZ, *a stern, bespectacled librarian*

EVA, *a brash, intelligent sex worker*

NEWS REPORTER

SETTING

The play takes place in a post-tech future at the City Hotel.

ACT I

SCENE I

Lights up. Some time in the future. Room 101, the City Hotel. Late afternoon. A suite that has seen better days: stains dotted around, peeling wallpaper, a carpet that looks as if it smells, etc. There is an en suite and a large window with a view of a brick wall. An air duct with a vent runs across the ceiling and a map of the city is pinned to the wall.

An old TV in the corner flickers into life. Static gives way to scenes of poverty and deprivation, before they are replaced by images of violent revolution and, finally, static once more.

After a moment, the toilet flushes, the tap runs and somebody screams.

VOICE OF THE ARTIST (*off*): Fuck! Fuck!

(*As* THE ARTIST *comes out the TV goes blank. He is barefoot and wears a paint-covered dressing gown that is too big for him. He is nursing his hand and has a cigarette in his mouth.*)

THE ARTIST: Fucking fucking fucking tap. Fuck! (*He sucks on his hand for a moment.*) Oh, sod it, I'll live. Unfortunately.

(*He goes over to stand by an easel and picks up a brush. He dips the brush into some paint without much thought, then stares at the canvas.*

He prepares to paint. Pauses. Repeats. A long moment passes. He doesn't move a muscle. He inhales deeply and is finally about to start when the door bursts open and THE MOTHER *enters.* THE ARTIST *puts out his cigarette and fans the air.*)

THE MOTHER (*impossibly quick*): The new management of this hotel is a shambles. I get back from a lovely lunch with the lawyer and they've forgotten all about my dinner reservation. No record of it, apparently. Nothing in the book, she said. Nothing in the book. Well, I said, if there's nothing in the book, that means I must not have come down earlier, I must not have booked a table for two by the window at seven fifteen and I must, on account of my great age and weakening grip on reality, be going absolutely, undeniably, irretrievably fucking mad.

THE ARTIST: Mother—

THE MOTHER: I'm sure the receptionist wasn't paying attention when I booked in. Daydreaming, she was. Daydreaming. Why do people do that? Night is for dreaming; day is for working. That's what I say. Unless you work nights, I suppose, but that's beside the point.

THE ARTIST: Mother, I'm—

THE MOTHER: Not that you can get any sleep in this city. Revolution after bloody revolution. Nothing changes. People on the streets demanding this and that, expecting the Party to budge or change their minds. No point. They never do. They like it when the people revolt; it distracts them from what's really going on. They'll be revolting against the revolution next. They were dressed up as gorillas today. Gorillas. Imagine it. The city streets lined with fucking gorillas. Well, they weren't actually fucking, but they might as well have been. Sorry, I shouldn't swear.

THE ARTIST: Mother, I'm working.

THE MOTHER: I shouldn't be so upset. It isn't good for me. I miss the old manager. Ever since he died this hotel has been falling to pieces. Have you seen the bathrooms in the restaurant? They're a disgrace. You've got to sit there and squat over a hole like some fourth-world savage.

THE ARTIST: Did you hear me?

THE MOTHER: I can't complain too much. It's not good for me. I must remember what the doctor said.

(THE MOTHER *pulls out some pills and quickly swallows a few. She does this again every so often.*)

THE ARTIST: Mother, listen.

THE MOTHER: Son, listen. I have just had the most wonderful lunch with the lawyer. He's certain we'll be able to put in a good case to the city board, and we could even have the property returned to our hands by the end of the week. I told him all about my plans for a café. I told him about that chap we know up north who'll front us the money. I even showed him my business plan – which he said was very good, actually, despite the fact that it was essentially unintelligible.

THE ARTIST: Mother!

THE MOTHER: What? What's wrong? What's happened? Where are you hurt?

THE ARTIST: I'm not – it's nothing – it's just—

THE MOTHER: You frightened me to death.

THE ARTIST: You can't keep barging in on me like this.

THE MOTHER: You've got to be careful. Remember what the doctor said.

THE ARTIST: What did the doctor say?

THE MOTHER: That you've got to be careful.

THE ARTIST: Sorry. But you weren't listening.

THE MOTHER: There's a woman around?

THE ARTIST: No.

THE MOTHER: You weren't masturbating again, were you?

THE ARTIST: No. Masturbating? What do you take me for?

THE MOTHER: A man? Oh, is there a man here?

THE ARTIST: I'm not gay. You know I'm not gay. I told you, she was a woman who just so happened to have a penis.

THE MOTHER: You need to calm down. I brought you some tea.

THE ARTIST: You know I don't drink tea. And what do you mean 'again'?

THE MOTHER: Nothing wrong with it.

THE ARTIST: I'm not saying there is.

THE MOTHER: Because there isn't.

THE ARTIST: I'm not saying there is.

THE MOTHER: Good.

THE ARTIST: I just don't like it.

THE MOTHER: Why not? Your father used to masturbate.

THE ARTIST: I was talking about the tea.

THE MOTHER: We all have our needs. Besides, it's good for you.

THE ARTIST: Please don't.

THE MOTHER: Remember our neighbour? He died because he didn't masturbate.

THE ARTIST: He got trampled by a horse.

THE MOTHER: Exactly. Just try it. For me, dear.

THE ARTIST: Oh, for fuck's sake!

THE MOTHER: Don't swear, dear.

THE ARTIST: I was talking about the tea.

THE MOTHER: We live in a modern world, after all.

THE ARTIST: Well, I sometimes wish we didn't. I miss the old days when we didn't talk about anything. No private stuff, no feelings, no problems. We were all much happier.

(THE MOTHER *hands him the cup.*)

THE MOTHER: The state of this city… Really, I think it was in better shape before the liberation. Yes, we were at the mercy of machines, but at least the machines knew how to pick up rubbish.

(THE ARTIST *takes a sip of the drink and immediately spits it out.*)

THE ARTIST: I wanted an espresso.

THE MOTHER: You've had enough coffee.

THE ARTIST: But I like espresso.

THE MOTHER: What's this? (*She gestures to the old map on the wall.*)

THE ARTIST: What does it look like?

THE MOTHER: It looks like you're trying to plan your escape.

THE ARTIST: It's for my work. It helps me paint.

THE MOTHER: Obviously. (*Looks around at the empty canvases.*) Barely any of it exists any more. Where did you get it?

THE ARTIST: The hotel lobby.

THE MOTHER: And this old bit of paper inspires you, does it?

THE ARTIST: Yes. No. I don't know.

THE MOTHER: You need some air. That's what you need. Fresh air. Let me open the window.

THE ARTIST: No, don't open the window.

THE MOTHER: It's good for you.

THE ARTIST: The only thing the air here is good for is sending you to an early grave. On second thoughts, it might not be such a bad idea.

THE MOTHER: We're ten floors up – the fumes can't reach up here.

THE ARTIST: No, don't – it's so…

(THE MOTHER *opens the window. The sound of the city fills the room. Loud.*)

It's not about the fumes!

THE MOTHER: I can't hear you, dear!

THE ARTIST: What?

THE MOTHER: What did you say?

(THE ARTIST *closes the window.*)

THE ARTIST: I don't need air.

THE MOTHER: We all need air, dear. That's science.

THE ARTIST: I'm perfectly happy in my own little room with the window closed and the world firmly shut outside. Sorry, but the quiet, and the old map, and the crippling loneliness – they help me think. Work. When I'm stood here wracking my brain for some idea, some inspiration about what to bloody paint, I just stand and look and think. And it helps.

THE MOTHER: Does it?

THE ARTIST: In theory.

THE MOTHER: So it's all for your pictures.

THE ARTIST: My paintings.

THE MOTHER: You know what I mean, dear.

THE ARTIST: My art.

THE MOTHER: Here we go.

THE ARTIST: Art. Not pictures. These are works of art specially commissioned by the City Hotel. They have to be brilliant. Each one must be utterly unique in its own way.

THE MOTHER: Don't get excited, dear.

THE ARTIST: Mother, please. This is my first professional job, and I can't afford to mess it up. The new wing is my chance, my opportunity to really make a mark. I know it's a mess now, but this place really used to be something. Maybe it will be again one day. Who knows who will stay in these rooms? Politicians, celebrities, art dealers. Yes, it's just a few grubby hotel rooms now, but if all goes well, who knows who could see my paintings?

THE MOTHER: Just get the job done so we can stay.

THE ARTIST: This is art, Mother. It's not just a job.

THE MOTHER: You haven't got to worry about it.

THE ARTIST: I'm not worrying.

THE MOTHER: I didn't say you were worrying, I said that you didn't need to. Nobody's going to look at them, anyway.

THE ARTIST: Excuse me?

THE MOTHER: I didn't mean it like that. That came out wrong. Forget I said anything.

THE ARTIST: How was it supposed to come out?

THE MOTHER: It's only a hotel room, dear. I don't mean to offend you, but people don't come to hotels to admire the artwork. They come to do other things. You know what I mean.

THE ARTIST: The birds and the bees.

THE MOTHER: Fucking, dear.

THE ARTIST: Yes. That.

THE MOTHER: Fucking.

THE ARTIST: Would you answer me a question?

THE MOTHER: If you asked me one that wasn't hypothetical.

THE ARTIST: What am I?

THE MOTHER: Oh, dear. Not this again. If you need to go back to therapy, I've told you, I don't mind paying. Whatever it costs, as long as it helps. And as long as you promise to try and keep your hands off the bloody psychologist.

THE ARTIST: Mother. What am I?

THE MOTHER: You're my son.

THE ARTIST: But what is your son?

THE MOTHER: I thought we'd sorted all of this rubbish out.

THE ARTIST: Just answer me.

THE MOTHER: Well. You're my son…

THE ARTIST: Yes, we've established that.

THE MOTHER: And I suppose you're—

THE ARTIST: Yes?

THE MOTHER: A painter. Obviously.

THE ARTIST: A painter?

THE MOTHER: A—

THE ARTIST: A? An…

THE MOTHER: An…

THE ARTIST: Ar…

THE MOTHER: An ar… It's on the tip of my tongue.

THE ARTIST: Well, stick your tongue out, then.

THE MOTHER: Oh, I don't know. Can I get a clue?

THE ARTIST: An artist, Mother.

THE MOTHER: Sorry, that's what I meant. Obviously.

THE ARTIST: And, please tell me, how is an artist—

THE MOTHER: Not a painter.

THE ARTIST: How is an artist—

THE MOTHER: Not a painter.

THE ARTIST: —meant to work with his mother barging in offering hot beverages and food every five minutes?

THE MOTHER: Oh don't be so dramatic. It's been at least an hour since I brought you your lunch.

THE ARTIST: I can't work under these horrific conditions! I'm sure being a mother is very difficult, and I see that these caring habits you have are lovely and have served you well for twenty-five years. But if I am to work as an artist – as a professional, a professional artist—

THE MOTHER: Not a painter.

THE ARTIST: Not a painter.

THE MOTHER: Not a painter.

THE ARTIST: I cannot have my mother barging in bringing me coffee—

THE MOTHER: Tea.

THE ARTIST: —and pastries every five minutes. Don't get me wrong, I'm grateful—

THE MOTHER: I'm sure.

THE ARTIST: Very grateful. But if you could hold off, just for a couple of days while I get these pieces done, it really would make me very, very happy.

THE MOTHER: Of course I can. Anything to make you happy. You need only say. I'll leave you in peace. To do your painting – sorry – your arting.

THE ARTIST: Thank you.

THE MOTHER: The bills I'll leave on the table. (*Goes to leave.*)

THE ARTIST: Wait.

THE MOTHER: Waiting.

THE ARTIST: Bills?

THE MOTHER: For twelve espressos, seven assorted pastries and one camomile tea.

THE ARTIST: But I didn't ask for any of that.

THE MOTHER: No. But you had it, didn't you? Just like you had my breast milk when you were a baby. Just like you've always had a roof over your head, dinner on your plate and a fire to keep you warm. Just like you've had my love and 'caring habits' for the last twenty-five years. Fortunately, the lawyer hasn't asked for payment yet, but I'm sure when the property goes through he'll want something for his troubles.

THE ARTIST: What about your savings?

THE MOTHER: Savings? What savings? There's nothing left, so you'd better bloody get on with it. We haven't got much time before the new manager chucks us out, and then we'd really be in trouble.

THE ARTIST: The lawyer has been working on this deal with you for months. You're saying he hasn't asked for a thing?

THE MOTHER: Don't call it a deal, dear.

THE ARTIST: Well, that's what it is.

THE MOTHER: That property was in our family for generations. When we came back to the city after the liberation, it had been taken by the Party with no regard to who it actually belonged to. I was born in that property. There is no deal, there is only justice.

THE ARTIST: Property? What is this word you keep using? Property? It's a little house! Just call it that. Property seems so cold. Heartless.

THE MOTHER: That's what the lawyer calls it.

THE ARTIST: Well, that explains it. Cold and heartless. Property. Client. Bill. I don't trust that man. I don't like his wonky eye. Whenever he looks at me it feels like he's looking over my shoulder at something behind me.

THE MOTHER: The lawyer has been nothing but warm and kind to me, which is more than I can say for you, you ungrateful little sod. Now. Get to work. Make sure you and I have somewhere to live at the end of the week.

THE ARTIST: Mother?

THE MOTHER: Son?

THE ARTIST: Before you go, could you look at these? They're the ones I've finished. Be honest.

THE MOTHER: How honest?

THE ARTIST: Just say what you think. But don't forget—

THE MOTHER: What?

THE ARTIST: You love me.

THE MOTHER: How many have you got?

THE ARTIST: Three.

THE MOTHER: And how many does the new manager want by the end of the week?

THE ARTIST: One hundred.

THE MOTHER: So you have three days to paint ninety—

THE ARTIST: Seven—

THE MOTHER: New pieces?

THE ARTIST: Exactly.

THE MOTHER: That's, what? Thirty—

THE ARTIST: Two point three recurring—

THE MOTHER: A day?

THE ARTIST: Yes. Thirty-two point three recurring a day.

THE MOTHER: And is that—

THE ARTIST: Possible? Debatable. But it has to be. Otherwise—

THE MOTHER: We're in trouble. Let Mummy take a look, then.

THE ARTIST: Please don't say 'mummy'.

THE MOTHER: Shut up and show me the picture.

(THE ARTIST *holds it up against himself.*)

THE ARTIST: OK. Right. Here's the first. It's a simple piece. I'd like to say it's formally impressionistic, with a dash of the contemporary neo-realistic movement of the East thrown in for good measure. (*He turns it around.*)

THE MOTHER: It's a pair of tits.

THE ARTIST: It's a pair of breasts, yes.

THE MOTHER: They look like tits to me.

THE ARTIST: The human form is the most natural thing in the world.

THE MOTHER: You're telling me they're natural?

THE ARTIST: They're impressionistic.

THE MOTHER: They look like a pair of fried eggs. Who was the model?

THE ARTIST: I didn't have one.

THE MOTHER: What are they based on, then?

THE ARTIST: My imagination.

THE MOTHER: Oh, my poor boy, what have you been getting yourself into?

THE ARTIST: They're impressionistic.

THE MOTHER: They're not based on—

(THE MOTHER *looks at* THE ARTIST.)

THE ARTIST: What?

THE MOTHER: They're not supposed to look like mine?

THE ARTIST: Yours?

THE MOTHER: Are they?

THE ARTIST: What? No. Don't be so weird.

THE MOTHER: Well, I don't know. You painters are a funny breed.

THE ARTIST: Artist. I'm a fucking artist.

THE MOTHER: Don't fucking swear.

THE ARTIST: Mother. These are not your tits.

THE MOTHER: I thought you said they were breasts.

THE ARTIST: Breasts. Breasts. These are not your breasts, Mother.

THE MOTHER: Good. Because mine certainly don't look like that.

THE ARTIST: Stop!

THE MOTHER: Have your tea. It's getting cold.

(THE ARTIST *takes the tea, sits and sips it. She picks up some magazines from the side.*)

What are these?

THE ARTIST: Just some magazines. They leave them in the rooms for people to stare at when they've got nothing better to do.

THE MOTHER: Why don't you use them? Like the old map. Find the nice bits, the pretty pictures, all that, and paint them. Your job would be a damn sight easier if you just copied.

THE ARTIST: I'm an artist. Not a bloody forger.

THE MOTHER: Well, you know what they say…

THE ARTIST: You can't choose your family?

THE MOTHER: Nothing is ever truly original.

THE ARTIST: Who says that?

THE MOTHER: *They* do.

THE ARTIST: I will not take somebody else's work and go around masquerading it as my own.

THE MOTHER: Everybody else does.

THE ARTIST: I am an artist. I have integrity. I am trained.

THE MOTHER: Partially.

THE ARTIST: Don't even go there. I was too good for that school, and you know it. I couldn't spend one more day there, listening to old farts talk about other old farts who painted even older farts. It wasn't an art school, it was a fart school, and I am no fartist. I am an artist. I have more integrity in my little finger than they do in their whole faculty.

THE MOTHER: You just showed me a picture of a woman's tits.

THE ARTIST: It's a *painting*! How many times? And they were *breasts*!

THE MOTHER: A *painting* of a woman's tits, then.

THE ARTIST: Thank you. A painting of a woman's breasts made entirely by my own artistic imagination. Do you want to take a look at the second?

THE MOTHER: If you're sure.

(THE ARTIST *grabs it and studies it.*)

THE ARTIST: It's what I like to call an amalgamation of the western expressionist movement blended with… (*He turns it around, revealing it.*) It's an arse. (*He stops and scrunches it up.*) Please. Just go. Let me curl up into a little ball and die in peace. We've got no hope anyway. We might as well pack our bags and go. I don't think I'll mind being homeless – it'll be a damn sight easier than this. Maybe I will join the Revolution. I'm sure they could do with some more cannon fodder.

THE MOTHER: Let me see the third one.

THE ARTIST: No.

THE MOTHER: I want to see the third one.

THE ARTIST: I don't want to show you the third one.

THE MOTHER: Why not?

THE ARTIST: I just don't.

THE MOTHER: Oh, go on.

THE ARTIST: If you're going to react like this every time I show you a piece, I don't want to show you. It takes a lot of courage, you know, bearing your soul like this.

THE MOTHER: It isn't your soul you're bearing, it's your sexually frustrated mind.

THE ARTIST: I am not sexually frustrated.

THE MOTHER: Show me the third.

THE ARTIST: Not a bloody chance.

THE MOTHER: I already know what it is, anyway.

THE ARTIST: Oh, do you?

THE MOTHER: I can make an educated guess. (*She points to her crotch and mouths the word.*)

THE ARTIST: What?

THE MOTHER: Vagina, dear. I bet it's a vagina.

THE ARTIST: No.

THE MOTHER: Prove me wrong.

THE ARTIST: No. Now, please get out. Out.

THE MOTHER: I can tell when I'm not wanted.

THE ARTIST: Oh, you are so bloody perceptive.

(THE MOTHER *readies herself to leave.*)

I can do this, Mother. I know I can. I want nothing more than to create art that is beautiful and honest and painful and resonant with the human condition. I want to make something great, I just don't know how to do it yet.

THE MOTHER: The human what?

THE ARTIST: The human condition. What it means to be alive.

THE MOTHER: I didn't know that being alive was a condition. Maybe I ought to get myself checked out.

THE ARTIST: Can't you see I'm on the verge of a pretty serious mental breakdown?

THE MOTHER: I'm just saying, you do sometimes make life a little hard for yourself. I'll let you know when I'm heading to dinner.

THE ARTIST: I thought you didn't have a reservation.

THE MOTHER: I don't. But I will. If the receptionist knows what's good for her. Will you be joining me?

THE ARTIST: I'll see how I feel.

THE MOTHER: You have to eat.

THE ARTIST: Thank you for reminding me.

THE MOTHER: And stop obsessing over women's bits. If you want a prostitute I can get you one.

THE ARTIST: A prostitute?

THE MOTHER: There's no shame in hiring a prostitute. It's like any other mutual exchange – you need something that somebody else can provide. That's how the real world works, dear.

THE ARTIST: You've given that some thought.

THE MOTHER: Oh, yes. The city is in my blood. Every last drop of it.

(THE MOTHER *grabs her shopping and her breather and opens the door.*)

THE ARTIST: Mother, would you mind bringing me another one of those teas? They're not too bad, actually.

THE MOTHER: Of course. Happy arting. And don't worry about finding a model – I'll find you just the girl.

THE ARTIST: No, Mother – you really don't—

(THE MOTHER *leaves.*)

—have to.

(THE ARTIST *lights a cigarette. After a moment, he rises and tears the first two paintings into small pieces. The final one, he reveals, is a vase of flowers. He compares it to the vase of flowers on the coffee table before ripping it up too. He stops for a second and sniffs the air. He can smell something. Not able to place it, he carries on. He stuffs the pieces into a bin, then disappears into the bathroom. The TV flickers into life. First there is just static, then various scenes appear showing natural disasters and the effects of climate change. There is a knock at the door.* THE ARTIST *emerges from the bathroom and the TV clicks off.*)

What is it now? If you want a drink, I haven't…

(*He opens it.* BEATRIZ *is standing there. She is carrying books, files and, of course, a breather.*)

Oh. Hello. That was bloody quick. Well done, Mother.

BEATRIZ: What?

THE ARTIST: You arrived very quickly.

BEATRIZ: You were expecting me?

THE ARTIST: Not expecting. More… dreading. It's nothing against you, see – it's just my mother. She has these… ideas. When she's decided on something it's impossible to get her to change her mind. Like bashing your head against an old, senile brick wall.

BEATRIZ: I don't understand.

THE ARTIST: Whatever she said, don't listen. She's getting old. Sick in the head. How much do I owe you?

BEATRIZ: Owe me?

THE ARTIST: Yes. How much money? You are familiar with the concept?

BEATRIZ: Of course I am, it's just… I think you—

THE ARTIST: Look, I'm working to a very strict schedule, and I'd rather not waste time debating at my door with some woman my mother has just picked up from the street. How much do I owe you? I don't want to haggle – just give me a price, a callout fee, or whatever. I can't pay you now, but I can write you an IOU. Have you got a pen?

BEATRIZ: Who do you think I am?

THE ARTIST: You're the prostitute. My mother sent you.

BEATRIZ: You think I'm a prostitute your mother sent you?

THE ARTIST: Who else could you be?

BEATRIZ: Do I look like a prostitute your mother sent you?

THE ARTIST: I don't know. I've never met a prostitute my
mother sent me before.

BEATRIZ: I think you have me confused with somebody else.

THE ARTIST: Oh. Right. Clearly. Sorry. You're obviously
not a… you've got books.

BEATRIZ: Can I come in?

THE ARTIST: Why?

BEATRIZ: I would like to come in.

THE ARTIST: Why? What do you want? I haven't got anything. Unless you want blank canvases.

BEATRIZ: You have what I need.

THE ARTIST: I do?

BEATRIZ: You do.

THE ARTIST: Are you sure?

BEATRIZ: Absolutely.

THE ARTIST: I'm flattered. What is it I have exactly?

(BEATRIZ *walks straight past him, inside.*)

Come in then, I suppose. Excuse the mess. The maid
on this floor has a terrible habit of not turning up since
she caught me painting in the nude. She screamed the
bloody place down. I did try and reassure her that it
was just red paint and not blood, but she wasn't having
any of it.

(BEATRIZ *takes in the room. She sits on the chair. Then she stands
again. All the time she is looking at everything.*)

So. What is it? Tell me what it is I've got that you're so
keen on getting. I'm dying to know. I haven't been this

excited since lunch. I must warn you, I'm already in the middle of a pretty big commission, so—

BEATRIZ: I've come to ask for your room. I need it.

THE ARTIST: Sorry, but, as you can probably see, I'm in it. So… no.

BEATRIZ: I need it.

THE ARTIST: I'm afraid I can't help you there.

BEATRIZ: I'll pay.

THE ARTIST: What's wrong with your room?

BEATRIZ: Nothing.

THE ARTIST: Does it smell?

BEATRIZ: No.

THE ARTIST: This one smells.

BEATRIZ: It isn't the smell.

THE ARTIST: I was going to speak to somebody.

BEATRIZ: It isn't the smell.

THE ARTIST: They're all the same, anyway, aren't they? Same carpet, same wallpaper, same view.

BEATRIZ: It's not the view.

THE ARTIST: Brick walls as far as the eye can see. Are you sure yours doesn't smell?

BEATRIZ: I need this room.

THE ARTIST: You can be honest. If it's the smell—

BEATRIZ: I must have this room.

THE ARTIST: Well, you can't.

BEATRIZ: Why not?

THE ARTIST: Because I'm in it.

BEATRIZ: I don't care. You can go somewhere else.

THE ARTIST: No I can't.

BEATRIZ: Yes you can.

THE ARTIST: Is there something wrong with your room?

BEATRIZ: Yes.

THE ARTIST: If it smells, I've told you, I've been having the same issue.

BEATRIZ: It isn't the wallpaper, it isn't the view and it isn't the bloody smell.

THE ARTIST: What, then? What could there possibly be about this room that makes you want it? I mean, look at it. There are stains on the walls, the carpet is like glue and it smells of… of… I don't even know what.

BEATRIZ: It's—

THE ARTIST: What's wrong with your room?

BEATRIZ: It's not the room I asked for.

THE ARTIST: Then talk to the hotel.

BEATRIZ: I've already tried.

THE ARTIST: I can't help you.

(THE ARTIST *opens the door.* BEATRIZ *does not move.*)

THE ARTIST: I really have to get some work done.

BEATRIZ: The hotel is the problem. I sent a message months ago to arrange a booking for this room, but when I arrived, they had no record of it. The receptionist can't have been paying attention. So unprofessional. The management of this hotel is an absolute shambles.

THE ARTIST: Maybe you ought to stay at another, then? I hear there's a lovely one just across the street. Tremendous views of this hotel's brick walls. Now if you wouldn't mind—

BEATRIZ: I can't stay at another. It has to be this hotel, and it has to be this room. I'm not leaving.

THE ARTIST: So you're going to squat in my room?

BEATRIZ: I'm not squatting. You let me in.

THE ARTIST: What are you, a vampire? Yes, I let you in, and now I'm letting you out.

BEATRIZ: I'm not leaving.

THE ARTIST: So you're squatting.

BEATRIZ: I'm not squatting.

THE ARTIST: You are currently squatting.

BEATRIZ: I am not squatting. I'm trying to explain—

THE ARTIST: I'm asking you to leave, but you're refusing. I can't move you physically, because then I'd be the bad guy. Who do I call? I'm getting somebody. Squatter control?

BEATRIZ: Let me explain.

THE ARTIST: Pest control? How do I get hold of them?

BEATRIZ: My father was Professor of Modern History at the Northern School.

THE ARTIST: I don't see what that has to do with anything. Unless he'll come and get rid of you.

BEATRIZ: Every year, he'd come to the city to work on research into the liberation.

THE ARTIST: So?

BEATRIZ: My father came here, to this hotel, and he stayed in this room, on this date, for a week, every year for the last eighteen years. But he died three months ago, without finishing his thesis. I've come here to do his work for him, and I have to do it the same way he did. To pay homage to him. He developed a relationship with another professor in the city, who, growing up, I heard lots about but never actually met. I've come here to find him and ask him how I should help him proceed in order to finish my father's life's work.

THE ARTIST: You've come to find the Other Professor?

BEATRIZ: I've come to finish my father's life's work. That's why I want this room. Your room. His room.

THE ARTIST: So you're not a squatter.

BEATRIZ: No. And I'm not a sex worker, either.

THE ARTIST: What do you do, then?

BEATRIZ: Why does it matter?

THE ARTIST: It matters because I'm asking.

(THE ARTIST *pulls his room key from his pocket and holds it up, like a prize.*)

BEATRIZ: I… I… I'm a bibliognost.

THE ARTIST: A biblio what?

BEATRIZ: A bibliognost.

THE ARTIST: Is that a skin condition?

BEATRIZ: I'm a librarian.

THE ARTIST: I've forgotten your name.

BEATRIZ: I didn't tell you it.

THE ARTIST: No?

BEATRIZ: What's yours?

THE ARTIST: I asked you first.

BEATRIZ: I'm B.

THE ARTIST: B?

BEATRIZ: Yes. Short for Beatriz. But only my parents call me that, and they're both dead, so—

THE ARTIST: Where's your room again, Beatriz?

BEATRIZ: Fifth floor.

THE ARTIST: Perfect.

BEATRIZ: So can I have it?

THE ARTIST: I can hardly say no, can I? Besides, it would give me a little distance from my mother. It's complicated.

She has issues with personal space. I'm pretty sure it's a form of maternal abuse, but I'm not certain. She hasn't tried to kill me. Yet.

BEATRIZ: Thank you for this.

THE ARTIST: No problemo.

BEATRIZ: It means a lot to me.

THE ARTIST: How's the smell in your room?

BEATRIZ: Why?

THE ARTIST: You don't like questions, do you?

BEATRIZ: What do you mean by that?

THE ARTIST: I mean you have glaringly obvious privacy issues and an utterly paralysing fear of being looked at for more than three seconds.

BEATRIZ: I do not.

THE ARTIST: Don't you?

(THE ARTIST *looks at her hard. After three seconds* BEATRIZ *freaks.*)

BEATRIZ: What? Stop staring at me!

THE ARTIST: Don't take offence. I'm not insulting you. You're weird. Weird is good. I like weird.

(BEATRIZ *freezes.* THE ARTIST *looks at her and smiles.*)

Come back in half an hour. We'll have to do it quickly.

BEATRIZ: I'm not having sex with you.

THE ARTIST: The swap. Why is everybody so obsessed with sex? My mother's out getting something to eat. I want to do it – the swap – before she gets back, so she doesn't know where I've gone.

BEATRIZ: She managed to get a reservation?

THE ARTIST: She can do incredible things, that woman. I mean, look at me.

(BEATRIZ *takes out some money and hands it to* THE ARTIST.)

BEATRIZ: For your troubles. I don't want any favours.

THE ARTIST: It's no trouble.

BEATRIZ: I want you to have it.

THE ARTIST: Really. It's no skin off my back.

BEATRIZ: Take it.

THE ARTIST: That's a weird phrase, isn't it?

BEATRIZ: Take it.

THE ARTIST: I suppose if I did give you the skin off my back it might be quite inconvenient.

BEATRIZ: I don't want to owe you anything. My freedom is important to me. If you don't take the money you're doing me a favour. If you do me a favour I owe you one. I don't like owing people anything. It's a rule I have.

THE ARTIST: A rule.

BEATRIZ: Take the money.

THE ARTIST: You take the room, I take yours. We're square.

BEATRIZ: I don't like that.

THE ARTIST: Why, are you afraid of squares?

BEATRIZ: Take it.

THE ARTIST: No.

BEATRIZ: Take it.

THE ARTIST: This deal won't last for ever, you know. Either we get moving, or that's it. No room. I can very easily close that door and keep it closed. Unless you're going to start squatting again.

BEATRIZ: You're being very difficult.

THE ARTIST: You're the one shoving money in my face when
I don't want it.

BEATRIZ: You're an artist. Don't tell me you don't need it.

THE ARTIST: Ouch.

BEATRIZ: Just take it. It'd make me feel better.

THE ARTIST: Look. How's this for a compromise? You take
the room, you keep your money, but to make things a bit
more equal, to keep your freedom, you help me.

BEATRIZ: I've already told you, I'm not having sex with you.

THE ARTIST: Just come back later and pose for me. How
does that sound?

BEATRIZ: Dodgy.

THE ARTIST: I've got a lot to get through. You'd be helping
me out.

BEATRIZ: I've never posed for anything before.

THE ARTIST: It's easy. Just stand there and be you. Be natural.

BEATRIZ: How natural?

THE ARTIST: You can keep your clothes on.

BEATRIZ: If I pose for you – if – I won't owe you a thing?
Anything? At all?

THE ARTIST: You'll get your room and keep your freedom.

BEATRIZ: How long will it take?

THE ARTIST: Half an hour. Then the room is yours.

BEATRIZ: And you're a proper artist?

THE ARTIST: Can't you tell? I've got a brush and everything.

BEATRIZ (*after a moment's thought*): Deal.

THE ARTIST: Excellent. You go and pack your things; I'll
meet you back here in half an hour. I'm going to order
an espresso.

BEATRIZ: You know, you shouldn't drink too much coffee. It's
bad for you.

(THE ARTIST *opens the door for her and she goes out.*)

THE ARTIST: Thank you, Mother. (*He slams it shut.*) Weird.

(*The door immediately swings back open and* THE MOTHER *charges in, brandishing a pile of files.*)

THE MOTHER: Guess what! (*She shoves her handbag, lipstick and breather on to the coffee table.*)

THE ARTIST: What?

THE MOTHER: Guess.

THE ARTIST: I don't want to guess.

THE MOTHER: Just guess.

THE ARTIST: Why?

THE MOTHER: It'll be fun.

THE ARTIST: The sun is on the verge of supernova and we have less than seven minutes to live.

THE MOTHER: No.

THE ARTIST: Shame. That would have been cool.

THE MOTHER: Guess again.

THE ARTIST: The revolution is over. The seas are retreating. Atlantis has re-emerged.

THE MOTHER: Can't you take anything seriously?

THE ARTIST: I take lots of things seriously. Coffee. Art. Sharks. I take sharks very seriously.

THE MOTHER: It's about the property.

THE ARTIST: The house?

THE MOTHER: The property.

THE ARTIST: I wish you'd stop calling it that.

THE MOTHER: The lawyer has informed me—

THE ARTIST: Informed?

THE MOTHER: It means told.

THE ARTIST: I know what it means.

THE MOTHER: He has informed me that he's found an error in the historical evidence that highlights, to a large extent, that the lease doesn't comply with the rules on Party acquisition of property.

THE ARTIST: You're spending too much time with that lawyer.

THE MOTHER: It means we have something. We have a leg to stand on. A leg. We have a leg.

THE ARTIST: That's good. I like legs.

THE MOTHER: I must admit, I was losing faith. I didn't want to say anything to you, but now—

THE ARTIST: We have a leg.

THE MOTHER: Apparently, when the Party regained control of the city deeds after the liberation, they couldn't understand any of it. It was all in binary. They made mistakes all over the shop. Just a bunch of ones and zeroes and no machines left to read any of it.

THE ARTIST: So the house is yours.

THE MOTHER: There are obviously many factors to consider. Many complex factors. Many—

THE ARTIST: If it isn't legally theirs and it isn't legally yours, whose is it?

THE MOTHER: Legally? Well. The Party are taking it into… they're taking the investigation… they're taking…

(THE MOTHER*'s mood suddenly shifts.*)

Bastards. They're taking it for themselves. (*She grabs a drink or three.*) The money-grabbers. I see their game.

Clear as day I see. This place... This city... Now I remember why I never came back. Nothing changes. Time goes on by, the faces change, but the people stay the same. They might as well be lining us up in the streets again and shooting us in the back like they did with the machines.

THE ARTIST: Mother! This is a good thing. I'm sure.

THE MOTHER: They're just putting me off, keeping an old woman waiting, hoping she drops down dead before she has a chance to fight back and get what she deserves.

THE ARTIST (*picking up the file* THE MOTHER *brought in*): What's this?

THE MOTHER: The lawyer gave it to me.

THE ARTIST (*reading*): '...the property now falls under independent investigation... The Party will hand over the case to an unbiased jury, who will investigate the case further...' That's good.

THE MOTHER: Independent? What do they mean by 'independent'?

THE ARTIST: I think they mean independent.

THE MOTHER: I wouldn't be so sure.

THE ARTIST: This is good.

THE MOTHER: They've still got to interview the witness. The lawyer and I are meeting with him tomorrow.

THE ARTIST: Where did you dig up a witness?

THE MOTHER: Here.

(THE MOTHER *hands* THE ARTIST *a picture.*)

The witness. He was a baker who lived near my home before the liberation. He knew my family. He fled, like us, but moved back after the liberation. We're meeting with him tomorrow to see if he'll testify.

THE ARTIST: He looks about a hundred years old.

THE MOTHER: Nearly.

THE ARTIST: Nearly a hundred?

THE MOTHER: Nearly right. He turned one hundred and three last week.

THE ARTIST: Happy birthday. Will he come?

THE MOTHER: All in due course.

THE ARTIST: He'll have to do it quick. Don't want him dropping down dead.

THE MOTHER: Although one hundred and three years old, the lawyer tells me he is still extremely lucid, healthy and—

THE ARTIST: Very well preserved—

THE MOTHER: Of sound mind. His memory is intact. Quite extraordinary, really. Considering his lifestyle. He's a fan of the drink, according to his nurses.

THE ARTIST: Nurses?

THE MOTHER: He lives in a sanatorium for the mentally ill, just outside of the city. Only a short drive from here. The lawyer is taking me tomorrow. He has his own private automobile.

THE ARTIST: If he is extremely lucid, healthy and very well preserved—

THE MOTHER: Of sound mind.

THE ARTIST: Then why is he living in a mental asylum?

THE MOTHER: Please! Sanatorium.

THE ARTIST: Why's he been locked up?

THE MOTHER: It was voluntary.

THE ARTIST: Why would he be voluntarily locked up?

THE MOTHER: You really must start using your head. In the city the average rent for a ground floor, one bedroom apartment is at least one thousand a month. The rent for a catered, fully staffed studio in the sanatorium is two hundred and fifty.

THE ARTIST: Ah. Clever.

THE MOTHER: That's an extra… what?

THE ARTIST: Seven hundred and fifty a month. What I could do with that… Think of the espresso.

THE MOTHER: Plenty for a man who has expensive taste in cigars, whiskey and women. The lawyer is driving me up to see him tomorrow. Now, I need to wash my hands. I'm not going to find any nasty surprises in there, am I?

THE ARTIST: Oh, yes. I forgot to mention, the maid is in the bathtub, but don't mind her – she won't disturb you, she's all chopped up.

(THE MOTHER *goes into the bathroom.* THE ARTIST *sits on the bed and picks up a magazine. The TV flickers into life again.* THE ARTIST *looks at it. It turns itself off. He reads again. The TV turns itself back on. He looks. Off. He tries to catch it out, finally giving up and flinging the magazine away.*)

Mind the hot tap. It's boiling. I burnt my hand earlier. I should sue. This is my career, this. My livelihood. Not that it fucking works at the moment. Stupid bloody thing.

THE MOTHER: Who was that woman?

(*The tap can be heard running.*)

THE ARTIST: What woman?

THE MOTHER: I saw her leaving as I was coming in. Ugly thing. Had books.

THE ARTIST: She was nobody.

(THE MOTHER *comes back into the room.*)

Wait. What about the tap?

THE MOTHER: Stop trying to change the subject. Was she a prostitute? I told you, if you need a woman I will sort you out—

THE ARTIST: She wasn't a prostitute. She was from the hotel.

THE MOTHER: She wasn't wearing a uniform.

THE ARTIST: She's off duty.

THE MOTHER: I've not seen her before.

THE ARTIST: She's new.

THE MOTHER: What did she want? If it was about the dinner reservation, I've sorted it out.

THE ARTIST: It wasn't that. It was about the smell.

THE MOTHER: The smell?

THE ARTIST: Yes.

THE MOTHER: In here?

THE ARTIST: Yes. The smell. In here. Like burning or something. Apparently somebody else complained. They're sending somebody up to… cleanse. The air. I've got to move rooms.

THE MOTHER: You're lying.

THE ARTIST: I'm not.

THE MOTHER: You're lying to me. Why are you lying to your poor old dying mother?

THE ARTIST: You may be poor and old, but you're not dying.

THE MOTHER: We're all dying. Tell me who she was.

THE ARTIST: Nobody.

THE MOTHER: Well, her very existence proves that to be untrue.

THE ARTIST: OK. You're right. She was a prostitute. I'm sorry I lied.

THE MOTHER: See, I can smell a lie a mile off.

THE ARTIST: I'm glad you can't smell it any closer.

THE MOTHER: You need to understand something about the city. The prostitutes here, they're clever. Very clever. They know how to get what they want.

THE ARTIST: Sounds familiar.

THE MOTHER: How much do you owe her?

THE ARTIST: For what?

THE MOTHER: For the sex. I bet she rinsed you, didn't she?

THE ARTIST: We didn't… have… we didn't do… that.

THE MOTHER: What did you do then, wrestle?

THE ARTIST: She's posing for me.

THE MOTHER: Posing? Is that what you call it?

THE ARTIST: She's coming back later to pose for me.

THE MOTHER: Nude?

THE ARTIST: Not all art is pornography, Mother.

THE MOTHER: Where have your paintings gone? I'd like to see them again.

THE ARTIST: I thought you were meeting with the lawyer and his wonky eye.

THE MOTHER: Purse. Left it up here. I'm meeting the lawyer downstairs. He's taking me for a ride before dinner.

THE ARTIST: He's what?

THE MOTHER: Taking me for a ride.

THE ARTIST: Stop saying it!

THE MOTHER: I've not been in an automobile for years.

THE ARTIST: Oh. That's the third time you've seen him today.

THE MOTHER: He's very keen on learning as much about me as possible. He wants to present a watertight case. Besides, I enjoy his company. He's a charming man.

THE ARTIST: You don't…

THE MOTHER: What?

THE ARTIST: Like him. Do you?

THE MOTHER: Of course I like him. He's a wonderful lawyer. We have a special relationship.

THE ARTIST: But it's not…

THE MOTHER: Come on, spit it out.

THE ARTIST: Romantic. Is it? It's not that kind of special relationship?

THE MOTHER: The lawyer isn't going to be your new daddy, if that's what you're worried about.

THE ARTIST: I wasn't worried about that.

THE MOTHER: The lawyer and I have a purely professional relationship. While the case is still active and he's representing myself in a formal capacity, there will be no – I repeat no – hanky-panky.

THE ARTIST: But after it's finished?

THE MOTHER: Goodbye, dear.

THE ARTIST: What about after? When it's all done? What then?

THE MOTHER: Must dash.

THE ARTIST: Mother. Answer me.

THE MOTHER: Have a lovely evening. Get some bloody pictures done.

THE ARTIST: Are you sure you'll be all right?

THE MOTHER: Don't worry about me, just get to work. (*She goes to leave.*)

THE MOTHER: Oh. Lipstick. Almost forgot that.

(THE MOTHER *puts the lipstick on, bags it and kisses* THE ARTIST *on the forehead, leaving a mark.*)

THE ARTIST: Mother.
THE MOTHER: Yes dear?
THE ARTIST: Breather.

(THE MOTHER *sees that she has left her breather on the side.*)

THE MOTHER: What would I do without you?
THE ARTIST: Die?

(THE MOTHER *hurries over and picks it up.*)

THE MOTHER: Remember, stay safe.

(THE MOTHER *takes a condom from her bag and gives it to* THE ARTIST.)

THE ARTIST: Why have you got one of these? Mother? Mother?

(*She leaves.* THE ARTIST *notices the lipstick on his forehead and goes into the bathroom. He runs the tap.*)

Ow!

(*The TV flicks itself back on. Loud. A torrent of disturbing images whip past, until it lands, finally, on a quiet and empty world, the world we know, deserted.*)

SCENE II

There is a knock at the door. THE ARTIST *sits up in bed. It is later now. It is dark outside, with the ambience of the city leaking in through the window. The room is tidier. Most of* THE ARTIST*'s things are packed away and ready to be moved.*

THE ARTIST: Hello?

(*The knocking is quiet, but grows louder.*)

Who is it? Mother? Mother?

(THE ARTIST *gets up and opens the door a crack.*)

Mummy?

(BEATRIZ *pushes past him and into the room.*)

BEATRIZ (*quickly – almost impossibly so*): I'm so sorry to disturb you. It's… It's… late. I'm sorry. Well, early, actually. Sorry. It's thirty-seven minutes past three. Or thirty-eight. Probably thirty-nine by now, actually. Maybe even forty. Sorry.

(BEATRIZ *moves around the room whilst* THE ARTIST *watches her.*)

I don't really know why I'm here, to be honest. I've been walking around the hotel for the last few hours thinking about… I didn't really know what to do with myself.

I had a few drinks, but I couldn't stand it in my room. I went down to the bar, but that was worse. Too many people. Too much noise. You're the only person I know in this place. This hotel. This whole city and the only bloody person I know is you. That's why I came. Probably. I don't really know what I'm saying. Sorry. I'm not usually—

THE ARTIST: Would you like to sit down?

(*He sits her down.*)

BEATRIZ: No. I'll stand. I won't be long. (*She stands.*)
THE ARTIST: I expected you earlier.

(*He sits her down.*)

BEATRIZ: I didn't… I'm sorry. Earlier on I… got a message… I mean… a telegram… my room… (*She stands.*)
THE ARTIST: Sit down.

(*He sits her down.*)

BEATRIZ: I'll stand. (*She stands.*)
THE ARTIST: Just sit.

(*He sits her down.*)

BEATRIZ: I'd prefer to stand. (*She stands.*)
THE ARTIST: Sit. Just sit. You're making me feel on edge.

(*He sits her down.*)

BEATRIZ: Sorry.

THE ARTIST: You don't need to apologise.

BEATRIZ: Sorry.

THE ARTIST: You don't need to apologise.

BEATRIZ: I'll sit. (*She stays sat.*)

THE ARTIST: Just stand.

(*He stands her up.*)

THE ARTIST: Sorry… I mean, thanks.

(BEATRIZ *sits.*)

BEATRIZ: I got back to my room, had a shower and there was a knock at my door and… and… (*She stands.*) I'm sorry. I'll go. You don't have a drink, do you?

THE ARTIST: I could get you a cup of tea from downstairs?

BEATRIZ: I'd prefer something—

THE ARTIST: Espresso?

BEATRIZ: A little stronger.

THE ARTIST: Double espresso?

BEATRIZ: I'd prefer a drink drink. A proper drink.

THE ARTIST: Ah. A drink drink. A proper drink. I can see what I've got. If my mother hasn't drained the room already.

BEATRIZ: This is stupid. I'm never usually like this. In fact, I would go so far as to say that I am usually, under normal circumstances, the least emotional person I know. I'm very good at managing my feelings. Usually. Usually.

(THE ARTIST *emerges with two mini bottles.*)

THE ARTIST: I have a bottle of—

BEATRIZ: Yes.

THE ARTIST: Or a bottle of—

BEATRIZ: Yes.

THE ARTIST: Which one?

BEATRIZ: Yes.

THE ARTIST: Right.

BEATRIZ: I'll pay you. Here. (*She reaches down her top.*)

THE ARTIST: Let's not do that again.

(BEATRIZ *stops. She takes the first bottle and gulps it down in one.*
THE ARTIST *wraps a dressing gown around her and sits her down.*)

THE ARTIST: I don't know how you drink that stuff. I had it once at a party and ended up throwing up in the punchbowl. To top it off, people didn't even notice. I couldn't bring myself to tell them. For two hours I had to watch people gulping down glasses of fruit punch and chunks of partially digested chicken pie.

(THE ARTIST *sees she has finished the bottle. He holds out the second.*
BEATRIZ *takes it.*)

BEATRIZ: Thank you. I know I probably shouldn't, but… Sod it. People do things they shouldn't do all the time, don't they? Why should I be any different? Have some.

THE ARTIST: I don't really drink any more.

BEATRIZ: Don't make me drink on my own.

(THE ARTIST *takes a sip. He coughs.*)

THE ARTIST: Lovely.

BEATRIZ: Forget about the room. I don't want it. No offence.

THE ARTIST: Don't worry. It's a shit room. That's just a fact.

BEATRIZ: Look at me. I don't even know you and I'm sitting in your room in a hotel dressing gown drinking your minibar dry.

THE ARTIST: I think it suits you. You're a little drunk, sad and feeling a bit hopeless. I think the only way to do that properly is in a hotel dressing gown.

BEATRIZ: This is totally ridiculous. I've never done anything like this before in my life.

THE ARTIST: I spent three years at art school. Well, two and a half. Don't ask.

BEATRIZ: I wouldn't. I'm in no position to be asking you questions about your personal life.

THE ARTIST: It isn't all that personal. It's just a sore point. That's what my mother calls it. I dropped out – well, that's not strictly true, but anyway. If I'm being honest, I never liked it. Too many fucking artists everywhere. My mother just hates to admit that her son, her pride and joy, has failed at something. I think she would have preferred it if I'd died. Some tragic accident. The more horrific the better. Kicked in the head by a rampant Shetland pony or something. At least then she'd have lots to talk about. And the flowers – she'd love the flowers. I can see her now, all dressed in black, the grieving mother. 'My son. The artist. He could have done great things. He could have been something. But he didn't masturbate.' (*He sniffs the air.*) Can you smell that?

BEATRIZ: You speak a lot about your mother.

THE ARTIST: No I don't. Do I?

BEATRIZ: My father was having an affair. (*Silence.*) After I left you I went to my room, had a shower, started to sort my things and then – I got a message. Remember the other professor I told you about? Well, they sent a telegram to my room. I thought it was his wife at first, but as it turns out, the Other Professor is a woman.

THE ARTIST: The Other Professor is a woman?

BEATRIZ: I had no idea. I was expecting some fat old bloke with a beard and thick glasses, like my father. Instead I get…

(BEATRIZ *gets out a picture. She hands it to* THE ARTIST.)

THE ARTIST: Fuck me. I mean… Fuck me, that's quite a shock.

BEATRIZ: I found that in one of his files. I should have seen it coming.

THE ARTIST: The glasses, though? At least you were right about that bit.

BEATRIZ: All those years. Lies. To me, my mother. Everybody. The Other Professor Who Is A Woman wanted to know what I was doing snooping around in my father's affairs. The university must have told her I was trying to get hold of his work. She asked me what the hell I was doing. I sent her an express message back. I told her who I was and… and she replied… she said… she said she had no idea. That he was married. Had a family. She had no idea I existed. Eighteen years he was seeing her, and he never once mentioned me. To top it all, she had no idea he was dead.

THE ARTIST: Did you tell her?

BEATRIZ: She thought he had run off with another woman. What else could I do? I polished off the drinks in my room, then I ended up here.

THE ARTIST: And you did some polishing here, too.

BEATRIZ: What reason would a man have to lie so much? I feel so stupid. It's humiliating.

THE ARTIST: We all have our secrets.

BEATRIZ: Yes. And sometimes they ought to stay just that. Secret. Eighteen years, and he never once mentioned me…

THE ARTIST: What about the work?

BEATRIZ: They finished it. Seventeen and a half years ago. I just left my job and travelled across the country to finish a paper that was published years ago. What the fuck am I doing?

(THE ARTIST *gets out a cigarette.*)

THE ARTIST: Would you like one?

BEATRIZ: I don't smoke.

THE ARTIST: That isn't what I asked.

(THE ARTIST *hands* BEATRIZ *a cigarette and tries to light it for her. It doesn't work.*)

BEATRIZ: Don't worry – it's probably for the best. You know, they used to put warnings on these things. 'Smoking Kills', that sort of thing. Now they don't bother. There's too many people, I suppose. Got to let people get on with it. Another death is just one less person to worry about. One less mouth to feed.

THE ARTIST: Thanks.

BEATRIZ: The stuff you learn about from books. It's fascinating the way the world changes. Like a pendulum. Before the liberation, everything was powered by electricity, everything was automated, run by machines, now it's like we're existing in some sort of purgatory, caught between the past and the future.

THE ARTIST: The way my mother talks about life before the liberation makes it seem like hell.

BEATRIZ: I think it's all a matter of perspective. Everything was perfect, you see. Humanity had reached its limit. We'd invented everything, conquered everywhere, populated the earth, we'd leaked into space, we'd got everything figured out. We'd come as far as anybody could imagine. But people get fed up. We decided we needed a little more chaos.

THE ARTIST: So they stopped warning us about cigarettes?

BEATRIZ: Exactly. They do all kinds of horrid things, apparently.

THE ARTIST: What kind of horrid things?

BEATRIZ: Oh, I don't know. All kinds.

THE ARTIST: I see.

BEATRIZ: Yep.

THE ARTIST: Well, cigarettes relax me and they make me feel marginally cool. I'll stop when they stop working.

BEATRIZ: And they stop being cool.

THE ARTIST: Which will be never.

(BEATRIZ *finishes the drink.*)

I could get you some more if you like? I'm sure my mother already has a tab. Or some food? Something to eat?

(BEATRIZ *says nothing.*)

Are you hungry?

(BEATRIZ *says nothing.*)

Beatriz?

BEATRIZ: I'm sorry. (*She gets up to leave.*) I should never have come here.

THE ARTIST: Don't leave. Stay. Please. You owe me.

BEATRIZ: Owe you?

THE ARTIST: You stood me up earlier. I got everything pre-pared. (*He gestures to the easel, which is set up in the corner of the room.*) I was ready to go, but you never came. I still need to get these pieces done.

BEATRIZ: I can't—

THE ARTIST: Just sit right there. Don't move a muscle. You look perfect.

(THE ARTIST *grabs his materials and begins to paint* BEATRIZ.)

BEATRIZ: What do I have to do? Just sit here or – I could go and change into something…

THE ARTIST: Stay still. I'll paint you where you are. Exactly as you are. Just try and relax.

BEATRIZ: The words 'just' and 'relax' should never exist in the same sentence.

THE ARTIST: Maybe think about something else.

BEATRIZ: Like what?

THE ARTIST: Somewhere you find peaceful. That some-times helps. If people are nervous.

BEATRIZ: I'm not nervous, I'm just… I've never done anything like this before. (*She closes her eyes and exhales.*) Relax. I'm in a library. Surrounded by piles and piles of books.

THE ARTIST: Try and keep your eyes open.

BEATRIZ: Sorry.

THE ARTIST: And if you could tilt your head… that way, yes.

BEATRIZ: Like this?

THE ARTIST: Exactly.

(THE ARTIST *paints her for a moment.*)

BEATRIZ: I hate hotel rooms… I can talk, can't I?

THE ARTIST: Course.

BEATRIZ: Spent too much time in rooms like these. Little purgatories. With a man, of course. I was working in a café during my first year at university, and he walked in. Older than me, quite a bit older. Mysterious. Before I knew it, we went from glances across the room to passion in fancy hotels. He was always gone by the morning. Work, I thought. Maybe another woman. I didn't care. The following week he'd be back in the café and the whirlwind would begin again. Until it stopped. He stopped. Weeks went by. Months. Nothing. I couldn't look away from the door. My whole life became dedicated to this man, whom I knew nothing about but loved more than I had ever loved anything. At the end of the semester, my tutor stopped me as I was leaving a seminar. A final warning. 'There's a time when the world stops rewarding potential', that was her phrase. Winter break came and I was running for the train back north when I brushed past a man. A man I knew. Except I didn't. He was dressed differently. His hair was longer. Beside him, a woman. Pushing a pram. We locked eyes. I'd never seen him afraid. I didn't know what to do, so I smiled and kept walking. What a cliché. I didn't go back for the second semester. Stayed home and lost myself in books. Spent so much time in the library they offered me a job there. That was ten years ago. (*She snaps out of it.*) I'm babbling, aren't I?

THE ARTIST (*without looking up from the canvas*): You have the most wonderful eyes.

(THE ARTIST *continues painting.* BEATRIZ *looks at him. Pauses for a moment. She stands and walks slowly toward him.*)

BEATRIZ: But you can't learn everything from books.

(*He stops. Watches her passively. She takes the brush from his hand and kisses him.*)

    Sorry.

THE ARTIST: Don't be.

BEATRIZ: It's been such a long time.

THE ARTIST: Me too. I probably won't be very good.

BEATRIZ: At what?

THE ARTIST: You know, the birds and the… fucking.

(BEATRIZ *moves close to him. She unbuttons and removes his shirt. He lifts the dressing gown from her body. For a brief moment they are lost within each other's embrace. There are noises outside.* THE ARTIST *pulls away.*)

    It's my mother.

(THE MOTHER *is tugging at the door handle.*)

THE ARTIST: Shit. I'm sorry.

(THE ARTIST *opens the door and* THE MOTHER *charges in. She's drunk. She is still wearing her breather.*)

THE MOTHER: Men! Men! You're all the same. Full bodied, empty headed. How could I have thought the lawyer was any different?

(BEATRIZ *gathers her things and prepares to leave.* THE MOTHER *grabs her.*)

They all want the same thing, dear. Don't ever, ever trust them. Procreation and recreation, that's all they want you for. Where is all the booze, and what is that ugly prostitute still doing here?

(THE MOTHER *glares at* BEATRIZ.)

Well?
BEATRIZ: I was just leaving.
THE ARTIST: Wait. Beatriz. Wait.
BEATRIZ: Thank you for the drink.

(BEATRIZ *leaves.* THE MOTHER *grabs* THE ARTIST *as he tries to follow.*)

THE MOTHER: Let her go. There are plenty more cows on the field.

(THE ARTIST *pushes her off, checks the corridor, then comes back in, slamming the door.*)

You'll thank me in the morning.

THE ARTIST: It already is the morning.

THE MOTHER: I am a grown woman, and I can do what I want.

THE ARTIST: I can see that.

(*Pause. She fumbles around, looking for her key.*)

So the lawyer wasn't…

THE MOTHER: What?

THE ARTIST: Nothing.

THE MOTHER: Good. Where's my key?

THE ARTIST: You forgot it when you left.

THE MOTHER: Can I have it?

THE ARTIST: Of course. Anything for you.

(THE ARTIST *gives the key to* THE MOTHER.)

THE MOTHER: Thank you.

THE ARTIST: You're welcome.

(THE MOTHER *tries to open the door, but she's seeing double.*)

THE MOTHER: Open the door for your mother. Be a good boy.

(THE ARTIST *opens it.*)

Goodnight, son.

THE ARTIST: Good morning, Mother.

(*He slams the door shut. There is a slight pause, then there is a knock at the door.*)

What now? If you want booze, I haven't got…

(THE ARTIST *opens the door furiously. He freezes.* EVA *steps in. She is dressed in long leather boots and a leopard-print coat that stretches to the floor. She flings her coat and breather on the bed and looks at* THE ARTIST.)

Er… Hello.

(EVA *puts her hand to* THE ARTIST*'s lips. She walks to the window and pulls down the blind. Blackout.*)

ACT II

SCENE I

The room. The blind is down, but there is light streaming in. It is morning, but has the air of a room that is trapped in the night before. There are lots of new sketches hung around the place. There is one painting wrapped in brown paper in the corner of the room.

EVA *is sitting on the bed and* THE ARTIST *is quickly drawing her with a new found fluidity and confidence. They smoke.*

THE ARTIST: I haven't worked this well in my life. You inspire me. Honestly, I don't know what I would have done if you hadn't turned up. Your presence. In this room. It makes me hungry. To paint and work and just keep working. I'm insatiable. Sorry. I know this is stupid. You don't understand a word I'm saying, but I'm speaking anyway. Nothing important, just… thank you. Do you understand those words? Thank you. Good. Yes. That is good.

(EVA *looks away.*)

If you could just… a bit to the left. Sorry, do you mind if I…

(THE ARTIST *touches her, gently. Positions her.*)

Perfect. Magnificent. You really are magnificent.

(*Pause. He starts to sketch again.*)

If I keep going at this rate I'll have done thirty in nine hours. Must be a record. Certainly is for me. Sorry – I'm just talking, talking, talking. I can't stop – stop, come on. This is stupid. You're acting like a moron. Don't embarrass yourself. She doesn't even speak… Thank you. Thank you.

(THE MOTHER *bursts in, wearing large sunglasses and holding a tray of coffee and pastries.*)

THE MOTHER: Good morning! I brought you coffee. It's so stuffy in here – it smells like a henhouse, but I won't open the window. I know how you feel about air.

(THE MOTHER *lifts the blind. The room is flooded with bright daylight.*)

You haven't got anything for a headache have you? I must have eaten something funny last night.

(THE MOTHER *sees* EVA *sitting by the bed.*)

Ah, so she's arrived.

THE ARTIST: You know who this paragon is?

THE MOTHER: Of course I do. I hired her. Yesterday. I found her on the High Road harassing an old gentleman in a horse-drawn Tesla. He'd obviously taken her goods, so to speak, and refused to cough up. Amateur. That's the first thing you learn. Always get the money in advance. Old boys are the worst – they've got less to live for. I thought she'd taken my money and run, but lo and behold, the prodigal prostitute returns. Better late than never, love.

THE ARTIST: She can't understand you, Mother.

THE MOTHER: Oh, yes, I know. I thought it best to find you one who was simple. A pretty little thing who'd help you get your work done with as little distraction as possible. I tried to get one younger, but she's the best I could find. Nicer than that thing you had here last night.

THE ARTIST: She's magnificent.

THE MOTHER: By the look of these, it seems to be working. (*She bends over to examine the painting now wrapped in brown paper.*)

THE ARTIST: Not that one.

THE MOTHER: Why not?

THE ARTIST: You can look at the others. But not that one. It's not finished.

(THE ARTIST *takes it from her and puts it back.*)

THE MOTHER: How many so far?

THE ARTIST: Twenty-eight.

THE MOTHER: In a day?

THE ARTIST: Eight hours and twenty-seven minutes.

THE MOTHER: And you say your mother is useless.

THE ARTIST: I've never said that. I know full well without you—

THE MOTHER: I'd have deprived the world of a wonderful artist and myself an ungrateful son.

THE ARTIST: You know I'm very grateful.

THE MOTHER: Do I?

THE ARTIST: I've never worked so well in my life. I don't know what to say.

THE MOTHER: 'Thank you'?

THE ARTIST: It's just coming out of me. Like a flood. Like a torrent. Like a… like a…

THE MOTHER: Whatever it's like, keep it to yourself. I've got a headache already.

THE ARTIST: What language does she speak?

THE MOTHER: Foreign, I think.

THE ARTIST: Whatever it is, I'm learning it. As soon as I possibly can.

THE MOTHER: Good for you. It's nice to have a hobby.

THE ARTIST: I must talk to her.

THE MOTHER: There will be plenty of time to talk when the job is done. Time marches on, dear. You've got to get us at least another week, otherwise we might be in trouble.

THE ARTIST: I haven't slept all night. I've just been working. Sketching, dabbing, stroking.

THE MOTHER: I'd rather not know what you've been doing with your hands, dear.

THE ARTIST: I've never experienced anything quite like it.

THE MOTHER: Well?

THE ARTIST: Well?

THE MOTHER: Oh, nothing. It's fine. I've spent the last twenty-five years expecting nothing in return, I don't expect that to change now. You don't surprise me any more.

THE ARTIST: Surprise you?

THE MOTHER: Just like your father.

THE ARTIST: I am nothing like my father.

THE MOTHER: I don't even expect a thank you.

THE ARTIST: You want me to thank you?

THE MOTHER: It would be nice.

THE ARTIST: OK. Thank you.

THE MOTHER: Excuse me? I didn't hear you. You were mumbling.

THE ARTIST: You heard me.

THE MOTHER: I'm old. My ears aren't what they used to be.

THE ARTIST: Your ears are fine. A little droopy, perhaps, but in perfect working order.

THE MOTHER: Say what you said a little louder so Mummy can hear you.

THE ARTIST: Please don't say 'mummy'.

THE MOTHER: Say it. Be a good little boy.

THE ARTIST: I said—

THE MOTHER: I got that bit. Carry on.

THE ARTIST: I said—

THE MOTHER: Yes, dear?

THE ARTIST: Thank you.

THE MOTHER: For?

THE ARTIST: For finding me a wonderful prostitute.

THE MOTHER: Good boy.

(THE MOTHER *kisses* THE ARTIST.)

Drink your coffee before it gets cold.

THE ARTIST: I wish you'd stop mothering me.

THE MOTHER: You'd be lost without me, dear. I know it, you know it, the whole damn world knows it. All young men who don't know where they're going, what they're doing or who they are need a good old spanking from their mother. Simple as that.

THE ARTIST: You never spanked me.

THE MOTHER: I was being metaphorical. Now, take this coffee. I'll only say it once.

THE ARTIST: You've already said it twice.

THE MOTHER: I can make the spanking literal if you want.

(THE ARTIST *sips. Spits.*)

THE ARTIST: Is this decaf? I'm not paying for decaf.

THE MOTHER: Consider it a gift.

THE ARTIST: A gift? You must have had fun last night.

THE MOTHER: Don't be a little shit. In fact I did. Last night I sang.

THE ARTIST: You what?

THE MOTHER: I sang.

THE ARTIST: My mother. Sang. How much did you drink?

THE MOTHER: Enough.

THE ARTIST: You sang? Ugh, the words feel weird in my mouth.

THE MOTHER: After dinner in the hotel, the lawyer took me to a bar off the Low Road. They had a talent competition. I was sitting at our table right at the back when, after an hour of listening to fools stand up, pissed, belting songs out at the top of their lungs, my name was called out. My name. I thought it was a mistake at first, then the lawyer gave me a look over the table. I knew then – I could see it in his wonky little eye – that he had taken it upon himself to test me. He wanted to see if I'd have the balls to do it. You know what I did? I grabbed my drink, a double, and I finished it off in one. I pushed my chair back, marched over to the stage and I sang. I didn't miss a single bloody note. You should have heard the applause. People stood on tables cheering. For me. One woman even asked if I was a professional.

THE ARTIST: A professional?

THE MOTHER: Well, I think that's what she said – she was slurring quite a bit.

THE ARTIST: I don't believe it.

THE MOTHER: Can you imagine it?

THE ARTIST: No.

THE MOTHER: It was wonderful.

THE ARTIST: And that's why you're pissed off at the lawyer? Because he made you sing?

THE MOTHER: I'm not pissed off. I'm just disappointed.

THE ARTIST: I've heard that before.

THE MOTHER: Men. All the same. Two balls, one dick, zero moral compass.

THE ARTIST: What did he do?

THE MOTHER: Nothing I can't handle.

THE ARTIST: You seem——

THE MOTHER: What?

THE ARTIST: Dunno.

THE MOTHER: Don't worry about me. The lawyer is a common breed in the city. Like rats. A new one shouldn't be hard to find.

THE ARTIST: He didn't——

THE MOTHER: What?

THE ARTIST: You know…

(THE MOTHER *looks at him and they exchange a silent word.*)

THE MOTHER: No. Nothing like that. A few honest words, is all.

THE ARTIST: I knew he was trouble.

THE MOTHER: We have to make our own mistakes, dear.

THE ARTIST: What about that man, the one you told me about yesterday? The witness. Weren't you supposed to be seeing him today?

THE MOTHER: I was. The sanatorium had to cancel.

THE ARTIST: Has he got something better to do with his time?

THE MOTHER: I'm afraid his time is up. The witness took his final breath last night, may the bastard rest in peace. He ate a bad oyster. He'd ordered a girl to come to his room for a midnight treat, and apparently it took her a whole hour to realise he was dead.

THE ARTIST: That's disgusting.

THE MOTHER: Apparently the girl insisted on being paid. She'd turned up and done what was asked of her and she wasn't leaving until somebody coughed up. The sanatorium settled his bill, but she kicked up an almighty fuss because they refused to tip.

THE ARTIST: A life of booze, sex and cigarettes, and what kills you a bit of bad shellfish.

THE MOTHER: I feel sorry for the girl. A whole hour.

THE ARTIST: How is it that she didn't notice?

THE MOTHER: Rigor mortis.

THE ARTIST: Right.

(THE MOTHER *lies on the bed.*)

THE MOTHER: I don't know. For the first time, I really don't know what to do. I'm going to dig around for another witness, try and find somebody else who can testify to something – anything – to prove I'm telling the truth. But I don't know if it'll do any good. I know I shouldn't say this, but maybe I ought to pack it all in. Maybe it is time to say enough is enough. They win. Go back north, settle down. I'm getting too old to keep fighting. I just want to lie down and close my eyes. (*Silence.*) Have you got a cigarette?

THE ARTIST: I don't smoke.

THE MOTHER: Are you going to give me one, or am I going to have to get up off this bed and find one?

(THE ARTIST *hands* THE MOTHER *a cigarette.* EVA *lights it for her and she sits quietly smoking.*)

I'm tired.

THE ARTIST: Why don't you take a walk?

THE MOTHER: No. I don't want to. I was walking around enough on my own last night after I left the lawyer. Bar to bar. Like a blur now. This city is falling to bits. Rubbish lining the streets. I can't tell you how many are homeless. Poor souls. This isn't the future we dreamt of. No. I want to be alone, in my room with the window open, staring up at the ceiling. Have you got any booze?

THE ARTIST: Should you be drinking?

THE MOTHER: Of course not. Have you got any?

THE ARTIST: All out.

THE MOTHER: You drank it all?

THE ARTIST: Not me…

THE MOTHER: Her?

THE ARTIST: Somebody else.

THE MOTHER: Ah. That's what you get for consorting with a bad woman. They'll bleed you dry.

(THE MOTHER *opens the door and* BEATRIZ *is standing there. She looks different.*)

BEATRIZ: Sorry. I've come at a bad moment.

THE MOTHER: No, no. I was just leaving.

(THE MOTHER *looks her up and down before slipping through the door.*)

THE ARTIST: Beatriz. I wanted to say… about last night… I… I… Can you smell that?

BEATRIZ: Listen. The Other Professor contacted me again.

THE ARTIST: The Other Professor Who Is a Woman?

BEATRIZ: She said she wants to meet me.

THE ARTIST: You should go.

BEATRIZ: Yes. Sorry, I shouldn't have come. You're busy.

THE ARTIST: No, I mean, you should go and meet her. You have to. I know that if it was me I would. When my father died he left us nothing. My mother, she changed. Overnight. She's such a strong woman, full of bite and venom, like a snake sometimes, which I love, but… but she grew old, so old, in a matter of days. Frail. I could barely speak to her. I still have a million questions I'd like to ask her about my dad, about what went on, but I daren't, in case she goes back to being the woman she was for those few weeks.

(BEATRIZ *takes a moment's pause.*)

BEATRIZ: Thank you.

THE ARTIST: So.

BEATRIZ: So. Thanks.

THE ARTIST: Last night. It was—

BEATRIZ: Strange.

THE ARTIST: Yes. But—

BEATRIZ: Nice.

THE ARTIST: Yes. Nice.

BEATRIZ: Weird.

THE ARTIST: Very. But—

BEATRIZ: Nice.

THE ARTIST: I'm sorry about my mother.

BEATRIZ: We can't choose our family.

THE ARTIST: Sadly not.

BEATRIZ: I think—

THE ARTIST: We should—

BEATRIZ: Forget?

THE ARTIST: No. Unless you want to?

BEATRIZ: No. Unless you want to?

THE ARTIST: No. Let's—

BEATRIZ: Talk.

THE ARTIST: Yes. Talk about… it.

BEATRIZ: Now?

THE ARTIST: Some time. Maybe not… also…

BEATRIZ: What?

THE ARTIST: That painting of you.

BEATRIZ: Oh. I hope it's not too awful.

THE ARTIST: No. It's… It's… I don't know…

(*Slight pause.*)

Where did she ask to meet you?
BEATRIZ: The Low Road.
THE ARTIST: Do you know where you're going?
BEATRIZ: Not a bit.
THE ARTIST: Wait there.

(THE ARTIST *rushes inside and grabs the old map from the wall.*)

Take this. It hasn't done much for me, but it might help if you get lost.

(*Pause.*)

BEATRIZ: Right.
THE ARTIST: Right.
BEATRIZ: Bye, then.
THE ARTIST: Good luck.

(*There is a moment where neither of them know what to do. She shakes his hand and goes.* THE ARTIST *goes back inside.* EVA *has disappeared.*)

Hello?

(*The toilet flushes.*)

Wait! Don't run the tap—

(*She runs the tap.*)

EVA: OW! Shit. Shit. (*She comes out.*)

THE ARTIST: Yes! Fucking yes! I knew it! I knew that the tap was broken.

EVA: My hand. I burnt it.

THE ARTIST: I told my mother, but she kept ignoring me. I thought I was going mad!

EVA: The tap. It's too hot. It's boiling.

THE ARTIST: I know! I burnt my hand earlier. Wait.

EVA: What? Oh.

THE ARTIST: You can speak?

EVA: Oh. Shit.

THE ARTIST: You… You…

EVA: Yeah.

THE ARTIST: Why did you…?

EVA: Your mother. When she hired me she told me I had to keep quiet.

THE ARTIST: That sounds like something she might do.

EVA: That was the only condition of payment. She said if I spoke it would—

THE ARTIST: Be a distraction.

EVA: Exactly. Apparently you're very easily distracted.

THE ARTIST: She seems to think so. I wouldn't know why.

EVA: I feel bad now.

THE ARTIST: You mean, you could understand—

EVA: Yeah.

THE ARTIST: What… everything?

EVA: Mmm hmm.

THE ARTIST: Right. Right.

EVA: It was all very flattering.

THE ARTIST: Yes. It was.

EVA: You have a lovely way with words. Very poetic.

THE ARTIST: Listen… what I said…

EVA: You don't need to be embarrassed.

THE ARTIST: I'm not.

EVA: I don't mind. Actually, I quite liked it.

THE ARTIST: You're not just saying that?

EVA: No.

THE ARTIST: Because I feel like a bit of a dick now.

EVA: Don't worry about it. I get it all the time. Really. You're not the first, and I doubt you'll be the last. Men seem to be utterly fascinated by me. I don't have the faintest idea why. Obviously I'm very sexually attractive, but I seem to have a strange effect on members of the male species. Maybe there's something in my pheromones. I've always wondered that. (*She pulls out a joint.*) In fact, I once had a man propose to me at a wedding. What makes that story so interesting is the fact that it was his wedding. I hadn't said a word to him. Never met the man before in my life. I was there for a job. His wife wasn't very happy. It was just, 'So nice to meet you – will you marry me instead?' Then his wife marched over and – SLAP! She had a terrible temper, that woman. Lovely legs, terrible temper. I feel sorry for her husband.

THE ARTIST: So do I.

EVA: Do you want some of this?

THE ARTIST: Is that—

EVA: Illegal? Not any more. Don't worry. Anyway, the smoke alarms in this place have been kaput since the liberation. If you'd prefer I could open the window.

THE ARTIST: No. Don't do that.

EVA: All right, bossy. (*She sparks up.*) You should have some. I know loads of artists that do.

THE ARTIST: No, thanks.

EVA: It might help with your work.

THE ARTIST: I tried it before, but I ended up locking myself inside a suitcase.

EVA: Rock and roll.

THE ARTIST: It was a weird night.

EVA: Have you got something I can… (*She holds out her hand.*)

THE ARTIST: No, you need to put it under a cold tap. But not too cold.

EVA: You know first aid?

THE ARTIST: I grew up in the south.

EVA: Country boy. Cute.

THE ARTIST: Do you think so?

EVA: Ropes…

THE ARTIST: Yep.

EVA: Knots…

THE ARTIST: You got it.

EVA: Trees.

THE ARTIST: Plenty of them.

EVA: What are they like?

THE ARTIST: Trees?

EVA: Yeah, I've never seen one in the flesh. Tell me about them.

THE ARTIST: Well, they're nice. I suppose. Very natural.

EVA: Elaborate.

THE ARTIST: Well, they're big and tall and green and brown and they have leaves.

EVA: But what do they feel like, smell like? What are they like to touch?

THE ARTIST: I suppose it's a bit like holding a really massive finger that desperately needs moisturising.

EVA: Right. (*She moves towards the bathroom.*)

THE ARTIST: So, are you really…

EVA: What?

THE ARTIST: You know… a prostitute.

EVA: A sex worker?

THE ARTIST: Sorry. A sex worker.

EVA: Why? Do I not seem like a sex worker?

THE ARTIST: I don't know. I mean – it's just…

EVA: Spit it out.

THE ARTIST: I'm digging myself a hole. It's just, you're so… beautiful.

EVA: Beauty is a funny word. You can look great, the world can adore you, but if you're rotten on the inside, there is no beauty. I am nothing special to look at. My tits are sagging, I've got bags under my eyes you could carry shopping in, but what I do have is a heart. And that's more than most people can say. I fall in love with every client I have. I need to. That's the only way I can do it. Night after night, day after day, cock after cock. I have to love them, because most don't love themselves. The beauty you see in me, it's not because of how I look. It's because I love you.

(*Pause.*)

THE ARTIST: Right. Thanks. I love you too.

EVA: You don't have to say that.

THE ARTIST: OK. I do like you, though. Quite a lot.

EVA: Thanks. Have you ever been in love?

THE ARTIST: Once. At least, I think I loved her. I definitely married her – I know that.

EVA: The first time I got married I was far too young. My father got himself into some big trouble with some very dangerous men, and the only way he could keep his kneecaps was if he gave me away to the boss's son. He wasn't a bad man. Good husband. Very sweet, actually. Lovely kneecaps. Until he lost them. No. When you find the right person you'll know. It may not strike you all at once. Love can be like a lightning bolt, but it can also be like a cancer. Something you don't notice until—

(EVA *slaps* THE ARTIST.)

That's it. No going back.

THE ARTIST: Are you married?

EVA (*giving him the joint*): Here. Have some. Look after it for me.

(EVA *goes into the bathroom. She runs the cold tap.* THE ARTIST *stands awkwardly. He puffs at the joint and coughs.*)

So, one hundred paintings.

THE ARTIST: Yeah. I've got until five o'clock, and I haven't a clue what I'm going to do. I mean, the ones of you are nice, but I'm not sure the new manager would be pleased to have your face plastered on every wall in the new wing.

EVA: I can't see why not. I think I have a nice face.

THE ARTIST: You do have a nice face.

EVA: Thank you. The new manager thinks I have a nice face, too. He and I are old friends.

THE ARTIST: You are?

EVA: Oh, yes. Before he got this place, he was running brothels on the outskirts of the city. Nice places to work, actually. He didn't take any shit, which is what you want as long as you behave yourself. Boys that didn't soon regretted it.

THE ARTIST: Yeah. I got the impression he was a bit like that.

EVA: Like what?

THE ARTIST: Volatile.

EVA: Volatile? Ha!

THE ARTIST: He sent me a finger about a week ago. I think it was a threat. Either that or the postal service has got even worse than I thought.

EVA: He's a businessman. Just don't disappoint him and he'll be happy.

(THE ARTIST *takes down the paintings of* EVA *that are hanging from the ceiling.*)

THE ARTIST: I think I got a bit carried away with these, really. It's been a while since that last happened to me. Usually I'm stood staring at the blank canvas willing for it to paint itself.

EVA: I know that feeling.

THE ARTIST: You do?

EVA: I know a lot of artists.

THE ARTIST: Old friends?

EVA: Exactly. This isn't my first time being a muse, you know. I've mused lots in my time. I've mused for the best in the city.

THE ARTIST: You muse very well.

EVA: Thank you. I appreciate that. You don't get enough feedback in this job.

THE ARTIST: Maybe you should get some rating cards.

EVA: That's not a bad idea. 'Number one sex worker, muse and professional badminton coach.'

(THE ARTIST *is still.* EVA *notices.*)

What is it? You look funny.

THE ARTIST: I've been thinking.

EVA: Never a good idea.

THE ARTIST: What if I'm just not that good? As an artist, I mean.

EVA: Don't be silly. You have a lot of potential.

THE ARTIST: There's a time when the world stops rewarding potential.

EVA: You're still just a boy. You could really be something.

THE ARTIST: But I can never seem to bloody finish anything.

EVA: Finished? Art should never be finished. It's an expression, not an artefact. Do you think the great Ardono took a step back from the portrait of pain and said, 'Meh, that'll do'? No.

THE ARTIST: But the great Ardono was mental. He painted with his own blood, for fuck's sake.

EVA: And look what he made with it. I've seen men do madder things for less. To finish an expression is to say that what you are expressing belongs in the past. That's history, not art.

THE ARTIST: But what if what I'm trying to express just isn't worth expressing? Isn't worth my blood? What if I'm one of those idiots who spends their entire life trying to accomplish something that is always just out of reach? Shit, I might be lying on my deathbed, looking back at a life of nearlies and close calls thinking, 'Do you know what? I would have made a brilliant doctor.' Beeeeep.

EVA: I think you'd be a terrible doctor. You think too much. You think like an artist, not a doctor.

THE ARTIST: You know a lot of doctors?

EVA: A lot of doctors.

THE ARTIST: Old friends?

EVA: Old friends.

THE ARTIST: Not that, then. Just something else. Honestly, if I thought I could do anything other with my life, if I thought I could be half as good at doing something proper, something worthwhile, of benefit, something normal, I would. I would trade all of this in a heartbeat.

EVA: Come here. Bitten off a bit more than you can chew?

(She stands in front of THE ARTIST. *She kisses him on the cheek and embraces him. The following builds slowly, but should be casual and easy.)*

EVA: Here you are, this young man, his whole life ahead of him. Slaving away in this tiny room, in this crumbling hotel, in this vast, sprawling city – trying, desperately trying, to make something of yourself, to create a life worth living. To be worthy of that elusive title – artist. When life, real life, life worthy of art, life of blood and sweat and tears, that life is out there – beyond these walls. On streets. Roadsides, rooftops. On building sites and demolition sites and sites of revolution. Where death walks daily. Where life costs something. Where life is a fragile thing that is fought for and won, not given on a silver platter. Not fed by mother to son with a silver spoon. Life is not here. All that is in here, my boy, is you. A boy alone, trying to capture on canvas a life you know nothing about. And think: you're not the only one. Far from it. You're just one lonely artist in a sea of many. There are hundreds, thousands of you all around the city, ceaselessly slaving away in your cages, wracking your tired brains for the next moment of inspiration, the next gift from the abyss. All of you wanting to create something new, something great, something big. When all you really need to do is open the door, step outside and stare open-mouthed at the world. Not for what you can take from it, but for what it truly is. A marvel. A miracle. A life.

(THE ARTIST *pulls away from* EVA. *He holds her at arm's reach.*)

THE ARTIST: That's it. That's it!
EVA: It is? What is it?
THE ARTIST: I've got it!

(*He kisses her.*)

EVA: Well, now I've got it too.

(*He pulls a hair from his mouth.*)

EVA: I think you've had enough to smoke.
THE ARTIST: Where are my shoes?
EVA: Are we going somewhere?

THE ARTIST: Not just somewhere! We're going out. Outside.
Out into the world.
EVA: Oh, lovely.

(EVA *finds* THE ARTIST*'s shoes and holds them up.*)

THE ARTIST: Bingo!
EVA: Now give me that before you wind up in a suitcase again.

(EVA *pulls the joint from him and takes a big drag.*)

THE ARTIST: Right. Come on. We haven't got a minute to
waste. Time marches on!
EVA: Rock and roll…

(*He stands up and spins her around before pulling her through the door.
As the door slams, the TV bursts into life again. This time, a montage
of dance numbers from classic films, interlaced with clips of warfare and,
finally, the birth of Frankenstein's monster.*)

SCENE II

BEATRIZ *enters. Lights up. Later. The corridor outside of Room 101.
The door is closed.* THE MOTHER *is sitting outside the door, holding a
bottle. They stare at each other.*

THE MOTHER	What do you want?
BEATRIZ	What do you want?
THE MOTHER	I asked you first.
BEATRIZ	I asked you first.

(*Pause. They hold each other's gaze.* THE MOTHER *wins.*)

BEATRIZ: I'm looking for your son.

THE MOTHER: He's not here.

BEATRIZ: How do you know?

THE MOTHER: Because so am I. (*Slight pause.*) If that's all?

BEATRIZ: No.

THE MOTHER: He hasn't got any money, if that's what you're after.

BEATRIZ: I don't want any money. I wanted to give him this. (*She holds up the old map.*) It's his.

THE MOTHER: If it's his, why have you got it?

BEATRIZ: He gave it to me.

THE MOTHER: Did he?

BEATRIZ: Yes.

THE MOTHER: What else did he give you?

BEATRIZ: Nothing.

THE MOTHER: Oh no. How late are you?

BEATRIZ: How late?

THE MOTHER: What are you, deaf?

BEATRIZ: What?

THE MOTHER: How late?

BEATRIZ: I didn't realise I was late.

THE MOTHER: You didn't realise?

BEATRIZ: What is it I'm supposed to be late for?

THE MOTHER: You're not supposed to be late for anything. That's why they call it late. If you were supposed to be late for something and you were, you wouldn't be late, would you? You'd be on time, and that's not late, is it?

BEATRIZ: What are you talking about?

THE MOTHER: Stupid girl.

BEATRIZ: Excuse me?

THE MOTHER: I will not.

BEATRIZ: What?

THE MOTHER: What?

BEATRIZ: What?

THE MOTHER: You're pregnant.

BEATRIZ: Pregnant?

THE MOTHER: And it's my son's.

BEATRIZ: Your son's?

THE MOTHER: What are you, an echo?

BEATRIZ: I'm not pregnant.

THE MOTHER: What do you mean?

BEATRIZ: I mean exactly that. I am not with child.

THE MOTHER: Are you sure?

BEATRIZ: I think so.

THE MOTHER: Well, that's not good enough. You need to check.

BEATRIZ: I don't think I do.

THE MOTHER: I don't care what you think. You've got to be sure.

BEATRIZ: I am sure.

THE MOTHER: But how do you know?

BEATRIZ: Because we never… I haven't…

THE MOTHER: You've never had sex?

BEATRIZ: With your son, I mean. I've had sex. Before. Just not for a while.

THE MOTHER: Well, what do you want, then? If you're not up the duff, what are you doing here?

BEATRIZ (*holding up the old map*): I just came to give him this back.

THE MOTHER: Right. Give it to me, then.

(BEATRIZ *hands it over, then continues to wait.*)

Anything else?

BEATRIZ: No.

THE MOTHER: Goodbye, then.

BEATRIZ: Well… Yes, actually. Do you know when he'll be back?

THE MOTHER: We've already established you're not pregnant. What else could you want?

BEATRIZ: I want to speak to him, I suppose. Yes. I do, actually. Yes. I want to speak to him.

THE MOTHER: About what?

BEATRIZ: What's it to do with you?

THE MOTHER: I'm his mother.

(THE MOTHER *looks* BEATRIZ *up and down.*)

Are you divorced then, or…?

BEATRIZ: I'm not married.

THE MOTHER: You're not very good at this, are you?

BEATRIZ: I've never been married, so I've never been divorced.

THE MOTHER: How old are you?

BEATRIZ: Why?

THE MOTHER: I want to know.

BEATRIZ: Well, I don't want you to know.

THE MOTHER: My son was married. Did you know that?

BEATRIZ: No. He didn't say.

THE MOTHER: Married his childhood sweetheart. It was doomed to fail. I warned him. After they were married for six months, she'd start to come home from work smelling of mackerel.

BEATRIZ: Mackerel?

THE MOTHER: It's a kind of oily fish.

BEATRIZ: I know what a mackerel is.

THE MOTHER: Then why did you ask?

BEATRIZ: I didn't.

THE MOTHER: Yes you did. You said, 'Mackerel?'.

BEATRIZ: Exactly. I said 'mackerel', I didn't ask what it was. I know what it is.

THE MOTHER: It's a kind of oily fish.

BEATRIZ: I know.

THE MOTHER: Well, she worked in an accounting office, miles from the sea. So it made no sense. Mackerel. In an office. Miles from the sea. One day, he wised up, and thought something was going on.

BEATRIZ: Something fishy.

THE MOTHER: What?

BEATRIZ: Never mind.

THE MOTHER: Anyway, he decided to follow her. Turns out she'd clock off early from work, drive down to the coast and cop off with some mackerel fisherman.

BEATRIZ: Oh dear.

THE MOTHER: She said she needed a real man and my son was—

BEATRIZ: An artist.

THE MOTHER: A painter. Exactly. She's living somewhere down there now. With her big smelly man. Unhappy as ever, I'm guessing. She always did have a face like a slapped arse.

BEATRIZ: This might seem impertinent, but, are you all right?

THE MOTHER: What do you mean?

BEATRIZ: You just seem a little…

THE MOTHER: What, because of this? (*She holds up the bottle.*) Don't be stupid. I'm celebrating. Can't you see how happy I am? (*She smiles, weakly.*) I am now the official owner of a pleasant two-bedroom detached house in the centre of the city, with a marvellous garden and potential for commercial development. It's everything I've ever wanted. Why would I be upset? (*She holds up the keys to the property and takes another swig.*) The lawyer dropped these off this afternoon. He'd been sitting on some evidence for a while. A written statement from an old neighbour. He was just trying to keep me around. String me along. He passed it on to the board this morning and they made their judgement immediately. Unanimous. Justice prevailed.

BEATRIZ: Congratulations.

THE MOTHER: I'm going to sell it. Move on. I don't belong here any more. I need a quiet life in the country. I thought I knew what I wanted, but I think I was just hanging on to something already dead. A past that I can never get back. We have to let go, dear, live for the future. We have to be able to let go of everything. Even our dreams.

BEATRIZ: Can you forgive?

THE MOTHER: Who? There's nobody left to forgive. They're all dead.

BEATRIZ: Can't we forgive the dead?

THE MOTHER: The dead don't need our forgiveness.

BEATRIZ: Perhaps you've had enough to drink.

(THE MOTHER *hands her the bottle.* BEATRIZ *screws the lid on tightly.*)

THE MOTHER: Perhaps you are a little impertinent.

BEATRIZ: But perhaps I'm right?

THE ARTIST (*off*): Oh, this city. This wonderful, disgusting city. I'm madly in love with the place. (*He enters. He is wearing a new suit and looks like a different man.*)

THE MOTHER: Where did you get your filthy hands on that suit?

THE ARTIST: Yes, the streets are lined with shit; yes, everybody is an utter bastard, but my word – what a marvellous fucking place. What an incredible city.

THE MOTHER: You're drunk.

THE ARTIST: No, Mother. I'm happy. For once in my pathetic life I'm joyously, incredibly, disgustingly happy.

THE MOTHER: You've been taking drugs. You're high as a kite.

THE ARTIST: High on life.

(EVA *appears. She, too, is dressed in new clothes.*)

EVA: I didn't give him anything, I swear.

THE MOTHER: What are you doing?

EVA: Time's up, I'm afraid.

THE MOTHER: Where did you get those clothes?

THE ARTIST: Care of the hotel. For delivering the work. One hundred paintings. A little extra because they were handed in before the deadline.

THE MOTHER: What?

THE ARTIST: You heard me. I'm done. *Finito.*

THE MOTHER: How on earth did you do one hundred paintings in five hours?

THE ARTIST: I didn't. I didn't have to.

THE MOTHER: I don't understand.

THE ARTIST: Turns out, being an artist isn't what it's cracked up to be. It's a lot of hard work, for very little in return. We have Eva here to thank for it.

EVA: I do what I can.

THE MOTHER: You're not even supposed to be speaking.

EVA: I'm no longer on your payroll, love.

THE MOTHER: Shut up!

EVA: No, you shut up!

THE MOTHER: What is this prostitute still doing here?

THE ARTIST: Mother, Eva is a sex worker. Not a prostitute.

THE MOTHER: What's the difference?

EVA: I don't know. The union voted on it. I don't care. You can call me whatever you like, as long as you pay well and don't try to kiss me on the lips.

(THE ARTIST *unlocks the door and they all enter.*)

THE ARTIST: Eva has saved me. She has opened my eyes to the wonderful world of commerce.

THE MOTHER: Commerce?

THE ARTIST: Money, Mother. Money. She introduced me to some of her old friends. Artists. Proper ones. Ones who actually finish things. I offered to pay them for their work. Turns out, as long as they get a drop of drink and enough cash for a few more, they're happy as Larry, whatever that means.

EVA: I know a Larry. Sad man. Chronically depressed.

THE ARTIST: We spent the afternoon collecting as many as we could, then brought them back here and handed them in.

THE MOTHER: This is outrageous.

THE ARTIST: This is brilliant, Mother. I'm going to be rich. You're going to be rich.

EVA: We're all going to be very, very rich.

THE MOTHER: You are just like your father. Why does possessing a prick make you act like one?

EVA: Tell them about the plan.

THE MOTHER: What plan?

EVA: Your son's staying in the city.

THE ARTIST: I was going to tell you.

EVA: He was going to tell you.

THE MOTHER: So tell me.

THE ARTIST: I'm going to start a dealership. I can work out of the hotel until business picks up, then I'll be able to get a place of my own.

EVA: I've already talked to the manager. He owes me a few favours.

THE ARTIST: The manager of the other hotel is converting the basement into a new wing. He's already asked if I can fill it. Two hundred paintings. We'll make a mint. Imagine it, Mother, you and I, a new life. In the city.

THE MOTHER: No.

EVA: I've got meetings lined up next week at every hotel for miles. There's talk of the economy recovering. There're rumblings that the revolution might be coming to an end.

THE ARTIST: In a year, every hotel in the country will have original works from artists associated with my company.

EVA: Our company.

THE ARTIST: Then we'll branch out – cafés, shops, apartments… not to mention the cream of the crop, which I'll flog at private auctions.

EVA: That's where the real money comes in.

THE ARTIST: This is it. I'm on my way. I've found my calling. I hereby renounce my previous occupation as an artist. It's too much hard work. From now on, I'm going to be the finest art dealer this country has ever seen.

EVA: Here. Take my card.

(EVA *hands* THE MOTHER *and* BEATRIZ *business cards.*)

BEATRIZ: Professional badminton coach?

EVA: Oh, wrong one. Here. Got these made up this afternoon. (*She hands out the correct ones.*)

THE MOTHER: You can't. You've been an artist since you were a little boy.

THE ARTIST: Mother, I'm nothing as an artist. I can't contribute anything worthwhile apart from tits and arses. You said so yourself. A product not of my soul but of my sexually frustrated mind.

THE MOTHER: I didn't mean that. I was just saying things. You can't.

THE ARTIST: This way I can help the real talent, the cream of this wretched city, to rise to the top.

EVA: And we'll make a pretty little penny on the way.

THE MOTHER: You bitch.

EVA: Excuse me?

THE MOTHER: This is all your doing. Women. This is the problem with women. They make you do things you don't want to do.

EVA: Would you prefer your son to have his head on a stake above the hotel? Because if it wasn't for me, that's where he'd be.

THE MOTHER: I forbid you to continue fraternising with this harlot.

EVA: Harlot?

THE ARTIST: The term is 'sex worker', Mother.

EVA: You can't speak to me like that. She can't speak to me like that. Tell your mother she can't speak to me like that.

THE ARTIST: Mother, please don't speak to—

THE MOTHER: Don't you forget why you're here, dear. Because I paid you.

EVA: And it's probably the wisest thing you've ever done.

THE MOTHER: No. You are an artist. You can't give it all up like that. For what? Money?

THE ARTIST: No!

THE MOTHER: A woman?

THE ARTIST: We're just friends.

EVA: I'm married.

THE ARTIST: Wait, what?

THE MOTHER: What?

BEATRIZ: You're married?

EVA: Of course. I love all my husbands very much.

THE ARTIST: I've made up my mind, Mother.

THE MOTHER: You've *lost* your mind, more like. Just like your father.

THE ARTIST: I am nothing like my— (*He stops. He looks at himself.*)

EVA: We've already signed a contract with the manager at the other hotel. And in case you haven't had the pleasure of meeting him, he makes the new manager here seem like a pansy.

THE MOTHER: How much are they paying you? It can't be worth it.

EVA: Can't it?

THE MOTHER: No amount of money can't be worth giving up your dreams for.

THE ARTIST: The basic fee is a thousand a piece. For features it's double.

EVA: And at the auctions, each piece will likely fetch anywhere between five and seven.

BEATRIZ: Hundred?

EVA: Thousand.

THE MOTHER: Well, maybe it's not such a bad idea…

(THE MOTHER *moves away from him, heading for the minibar.*)

BEATRIZ: I met her.

THE ARTIST: Who? The Other Professor Who Is a Woman?

BEATRIZ: We chatted all afternoon. I could hardly believe it. We drank coffee. Ate pastries. Talked about family. My family. Her family. My father. She showed me things. Pictures. The years they shared. They were very, very happy together.

THE ARTIST: And now? What will you do? Are you staying?

BEATRIZ: My train back north leaves in an hour. Here, you better have this. (*She hands over the old map.*) I think I can find my own way now. It really was lovely to meet you. Thank you so much for everything. Good luck. I hope you find happiness. Or something like it.

(*They are still for a moment.*)

THE ARTIST: Last night. Us. The kiss. I wanted to say… I wanted to tell you… I wanted to show you the painting.

BEATRIZ: You're not really going to give it all up, are you?

THE ARTIST: What do you mean?

BEATRIZ: The art. Your dream.

THE ARTIST: I was wrong, Beatriz. I'm not an artist.

BEATRIZ: The first thing I thought when I met you was how wonderful it must feel to know what you want. Out of everything in the world, to have a dream, something to live for. To hear you say that you'll give it up to get people off your back, to make money, it's… heartbreaking.

(THE MOTHER *sees a painting still sitting on the floor. It is wrapped in brown paper. She picks it up.*)

THE MOTHER: Son.
THE ARTIST: One minute, Mother.
THE MOTHER: I thought you said you'd taken all the paintings down already.
THE ARTIST: I have.
THE MOTHER: What's that, then?
THE ARTIST: Oh. That's… It's nothing.

(THE MOTHER *goes to grab it.*)

   Don't touch it!
THE MOTHER: Why not?
THE ARTIST: I…
EVA: Why not?
THE ARTIST: It's…
BEATRIZ: Why not?
THE ARTIST: It's not… It's rubbish. I was about to bin it. Honestly, don't.
THE MOTHER: Let me take a look.
THE ARTIST: No. Please, Mother.
THE MOTHER: You.
EVA: What?
THE MOTHER: Hold him.
EVA: What?
THE ARTIST: What?
BEATRIZ: What?
THE MOTHER: Did I mumble? Hold him.
EVA: OK, bossy.

(EVA *grabs* THE ARTIST *and holds him tight.*)

THE ARTIST: Ow! Eva. Mother, please. Don't. Just leave it. Just leave it! It's… not… It's not…

(THE MOTHER *places it on an easel and rips open the paper.*)

Mother!

(*Silence.*)

THE MOTHER: Son.

(EVA *lets go of him and goes to the painting.*)

BEATRIZ: Oh my.
EVA: Oh my fuck.
THE MOTHER: Oh. My boy.
THE ARTIST: What? It's terrible, isn't it? I knew I should have thrown it away when I had the chance.

(*Smoke begins to pour from the air vent. They continue to stare at the painting.*)

EVA: It's…
THE ARTIST: What?
EVA: It's…
BEATRIZ: It's…
EVA: It's…
BEATRIZ: It's me.
THE MOTHER: It is the most beautiful thing I have ever seen.

(*Silence. They all stare, transfixed, at the painting as it glows.* THE ARTIST *rises to his feet. He stops. Stares at the painting.* EVA *sniffs. So does* THE MOTHER. *So does* BEATRIZ.)

EVA: What's that smell?

(*They see the smoke, now beginning to fill the room. The lights in the room turn on for the first time. A fire alarm goes off in the corridor. The TV bursts into life. Static, loud.*)

THE MOTHER: What the hell is that?
EVA: The power. The power is back on.
THE MOTHER: It's impossible.

(*A sprinkler suddenly turns on and water hits the painting, ruining it.*)

THE ARTIST: No!

(*There is a deep rumbling noise.*)

EVA: Can you feel that? The building is shaking.
THE MOTHER: The whole thing is coming down.

(EVA *and* THE MOTHER *hurriedly make their way out.* EVA *heads for the window. As she opens it, the sound of a city descending into chaos spills inside. She cocks her leg over the windowsill. The smoke grows thicker. The building shakes. The TV suddenly grows louder and scenes of joyous celebration begin to play. Over the top, a* NEWS REPORTER *can be heard.*)

NEWS REPORTER: Good evening, I'm broadcasting live from the centre of the city. For the first time in over a decade,

the power has been restored and I am able to communic-
ate live over the airwaves. It is official. The news is out.
The King is dead. I repeat, the King is dead. The revolution is over. In other news, scientists have announced that
after over a century of climate change, seas appear to be
retreating, and even Atlantis, a city that has been lost for
millennia, has begun to re-emerge…

(BEATRIZ *turns and sees* THE ARTIST, *still staring, oblivious.*)

BEATRIZ: Wait.

THE MOTHER: What are you doing? Don't just stand there.

BEATRIZ: We've got to go.

THE MOTHER: This place is falling to the ground. We've got
    to get out. Now.

EVA: Leave him. He's an artist.

THE MOTHER: What the hell does that mean?

EVA: I don't know. Just thought it was the right moment for a
    grand romantic gesture.

THE MOTHER: Oh, come on! It doesn't matter now!

(EVA *is nearly out of the window.* THE MOTHER *is halfway through.*)

It isn't worth dying for!

(THE ARTIST *remains still, looking on in horror.* BEATRIZ *goes to him
and takes his hand.*)

BEATRIZ (*shouting*): I'm pregnant!

(*They all stop.* THE ARTIST *looks at her.*)

THE ARTIST: What?

EVA: Congratulations!

THE MOTHER: I knew it!

BEATRIZ: I'm not really, I just needed to get your attention. We've got to go. We've got to leave. It's over. You can do another painting. I'll pose for you again. It's gone. It's gone.

THE ARTIST: The only thing I've ever finished. And it's gone. For ever.

(The water continues to fall. A cacophony of sound. The world crumbling to dust.)

It was good, wasn't it?

BEATRIZ: It was good. It was good.

(THE ARTIST gets out a cigarette and tries to light it. It doesn't work. He takes it out of his mouth and snaps it in two. Then there is silence. The room darkens until only THE ARTIST and the painting are lit. He stares at the now blank canvas.)

Oh well.

(Blackout.)